But . . .

continued on page 94

3

£3.25

CON

PAGE 29

PAGE 45

PAGE 17

4

TENTS

PAGE 78

PAGE 52

Printed and Published in Great Britain by D. C. THOMSON & CO., LTD., 185 Fleet Street, London EC4A 2HS.
© D. C. THOMSON & CO., LTD., 1989.
ISBN 0-85116-443-9

5

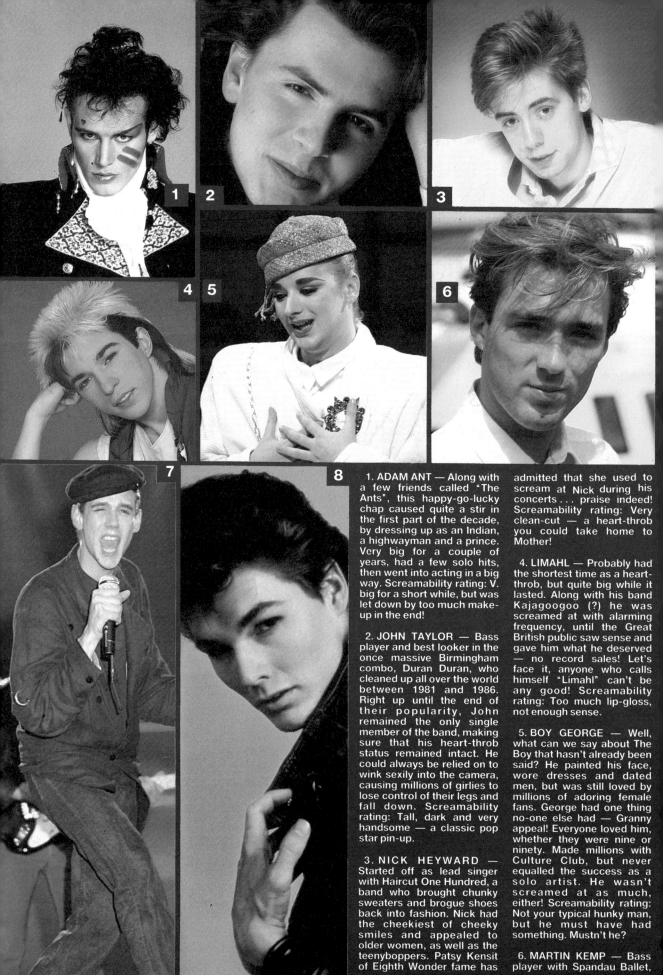

1. ADAM ANT — Along with a few friends called "The Ants", this happy-go-lucky chap caused quite a stir in the first part of the decade, by dressing up as an Indian, a highwayman and a prince. Very big for a couple of years, had a few solo hits, then went into acting in a big way. Screamability rating: V. big for a short while, but was let down by too much make-up in the end!

2. JOHN TAYLOR — Bass player and best looker in the once massive Birmingham combo, Duran Duran, who cleaned up all over the world between 1981 and 1986. Right up until the end of their popularity, John remained the only single member of the band, making sure that his heart-throb status remained intact. He could always be relied on to wink sexily into the camera, causing millions of girlies to lose control of their legs and fall down. Screamability rating: Tall, dark and very handsome — a classic pop star pin-up.

3. NICK HEYWARD — Started off as lead singer with Haircut One Hundred, a band who brought chunky sweaters and brogue shoes back into fashion. Nick had the cheekiest of cheeky smiles and appealed to older women, as well as the teenyboppers. Patsy Kensit of Eighth Wonder fame has admitted that she used to scream at Nick during his concerts . . . praise indeed! Screamability rating: Very clean-cut — a heart-throb you could take home to Mother!

4. LIMAHL — Probably had the shortest time as a heart-throb, but quite big while it lasted. Along with his band Kajagoogoo (?) he was screamed at with alarming frequency, until the Great British public saw sense and gave him what he deserved — no record sales! Let's face it, anyone who calls himself "Limahl" can't be any good! Screamability rating: Too much lip-gloss, not enough sense.

5. BOY GEORGE — Well, what can we say about The Boy that hasn't already been said? He painted his face, wore dresses and dated men, but was still loved by millions of adoring female fans. George had one thing no-one else had — Granny appeal! Everyone loved him, whether they were nine or ninety. Made millions with Culture Club, but never equalled the success as a solo artist. He wasn't screamed at as much, either! Screamability rating: Not your typical hunky man, but he must have had something. Mustn't he?

6. MARTIN KEMP — Bass player with Spandau Ballet,

THE DIRTY DOZEN...
MINUS TWO!

Patches has a look back at the 10 biggest heart-throbs of the last decade. We think there'll be at least one here that has appeared on your bedroom wall sometime during the 80's!

9

10

one of the most popular bands of the decade. His appeal was his old-fashioned, macho good looks, along with the fact that he was known as a bit of an, ahem, lad with the ladies! His brother Gary (Spandau's guitarist) never managed to equal Martin's popularity, but did OK! Screamability rating: Very much in the John Taylor mould — a good, old-fashioned heart-throb.

7. BEN VOLPELIERE-PIERROT — Lead singer and knee-bender with Curiosity Killed The Cat. Thing is, he didn't have a lot going for him — he was balding, spotty and couldn't dance. However, rarely has someone been screamed at as much as Ben. Also, rarely has a heart-throb's career been so short-lived as Ben's. Shame, really. Screamability rating: A flash in the pan.

8. MORTEN HARKET — The boy next door! This is the only pin-up who looked like a foreign-exchange student! Morten had it all ... the cheekbones, the hair gel and the high voice — he had it made from the start, but was never very happy with the heart-throb label. His band A-ha made great pop songs, along with superb videos which showed Morten off to a tee. He did lose marks for his dress

sense, though — denim ... denim ... denim — a bit like Shakin' Stevens with a Norwegian accent! Screamability rating: Not exactly macho, but quite similar to the Nick Heyward appeal.

9. MARTI PELLOW — Or, how a brickie from Glasgow can become a legend in 10 easy lessons. First, smile a lot. Second, wear a lot of hair gel. Thirdly, have a lot of hit records ... etc! Marti was always just like you'd expect him to be — down to earth, very Glaswegian and rich! He had what could be described as a truly great voice — his biggest rivals were Bros, whose fans hated Wet Wet Wet fans with a passion! Screamability rating: Just made to adorn magazine covers everywhere!

10. MATT GOSS — Lead singer with one of the biggest teen sensations of the decade ... Bros! Matt had the looks of James Dean and the voice of Michael Jackson — sheer perfection! He and the rest of Bros were chased, mobbed, screamed at and thoroughly adored by thousands of girls all over the place. Nuff said! Screamability rating: one of the biggest heart-throbs of the decade. Made ripped jeans and Doc Martens fashionable ... he does have a lot to answer for!

CHOICES CH

WHAT we want to do is to give you some help with your choice of careers — outline some of the most popular jobs for girls, and some of the less traditional ones that may interest you, as well as telling you what sorts of qualifications and qualities your employers will want you to have.

Recently, there was a study done in America to find out just how many jobs there were in the world. What they were trying to find out was what sort of range of occupations there were. It may come as a surprise to you that there are over 400,000 different types of jobs to choose from throughout the world! Of course, there aren't going to be nearly that many in Britain, so you'll just have to make do with a few thousand! Before you take the plunge and choose what you want to do with your life, a good idea is to find out just what kind of person you are. What you're like will probably affect your choice of subjects and the type of work you'll be interested in. For many jobs, what you are like as a person is as important as the qualifications that you attain in school or further education. You may have GCSEs or 'O'-Grades up the Ying-Yang, but you may also be totally unsuited to the job. For example, can you imagine having all the qualifications to be a teacher and hating children? Or wanting to be a doctor, when you can't stand the sight of blood?

When you're thinking about possible types of careers that could interest you, remember the following:

Try to list all the personal qualities needed in those jobs. Try to be honest with yourself and see if you have those qualities.

Ask yourself what you could do to develop the right kind of personal qualities for jobs that interest you.

Ask your friends and family if they think you are the type of person who is suited to the kind of occupation you have in mind.

If you don't think you match the job, but are still interested, ask yourself whether in time you could develop the qualities needed, because people *can* change.

For many of you, the time will soon arrive when you have to choose the subjects that you'll be studying as part of your GCSEs or 'O'-Grades, if you live in Scotland.
It *is* a very confusing and worrying time for a lot of people . . .
Will I be able to do what I want to do with these subjects?
I don't know what I want to do as a career, so what subjects do I choose?
What happens if I choose these subjects, and then change my mind in a year?

JOB FAMILIES

Sometimes it's not a good idea to be too specific when you're thinking about possible careers. If you gear yourself all towards one job in particular, you may find that you change your mind halfway through your course — and then you're stuck. After all, just think of the amount of times you've changed your mind about subjects all the way through your life — does this sound familiar?

"Oh, Mum — I've just *got* to have that new bike for Christmas. Forget what I said last week about the video game, and what I said last month about the puppy dog. I really, really want this bike. OK?"

Of course, we've all done it — it's all part of our development. So, if we're always going to change our minds about things, why should careers be any different? Remember that, from the time you make your subject choice, you're going to have at least 4 or 5 years before you, hopefully, begin that particular career. Just think how many times you'll change your mind about your favourite pop group in that time!

So, a better idea than focusing on one specific career would seem to be more wide ranging, to give yourself more room for scope, or changing your mind. A perfect way to do this is to use what are called The Job Families.

There are six job families, and they can be described like this.
1. Creative
2. Scientific and working with numbers
3. Outdoor
4. Working with or caring for people
5. Practical
6. Continuing with education or training

Each family contains many different specific jobs. For instance, jobs like acting, music, writing, etc., are included in the Creative section. Accountancy, dentistry, and medicine are part of the second family. If you fancy the great outdoors, then jobs such as farm work, forestry and veterinary work are next. The fourth family — Caring for and working with people — has an enormous amount of people involved in its related jobs. Nursery nurse, teacher, police officer or fire

OICES CHOICES

fighter are all jobs that fall into this category. You would think that the practical family would appeal more to boys, but jobs such as sewing machinist and cook are also included, as well as the more traditionally male occupations of plumber, motor mechanic and joiner. Rules, however, are made to be broken — if you want to be a motor mechanic, the only thing that stands in your way is your own indecision or lack of confidence.

The last group deals with all those people who choose to continue their education in university or college, before they start working in a chosen career, or go into fifth and sixth form college. Or start on a government training programme, such as the Youth Training Scheme (YTS).

Try to find out what *family* interests you, then you'll be able (without too much difficulty) to change to another, similar job if your chances for one falls through, or you don't get the required qualifications. However, just to give you an idea of what the qualifications situation is, we'll outline a few popular jobs, and what sort of exam results you'll need, as well as the personal qualities that'll be required:

Fashion Designer:

May work on mens or womens clothing, fashion accessories, lingerie, shoes, etc. Most designers start with a formal training such as a BTEC/ SCOTVEC course or a degree.

Hairdresser:

All aspects of hair care work included. Must enjoy dealing with people. Apprenticeship course available at some colleges and salons. GSCE/ SCE English and science subjects an advantage. High percentage of those who enter this field do so through the YTS.

Teacher:

May work in colleges of further or higher education, polytechnics or universities, as well as primary and secondary schools. A degree is demanded for this one.

Bank Clerk:

Minimum four GSCE/SCE 'O'-grades/'S'-grades preferably including English and a subject that shows you can handle numbers. Passes at 'A'-level/'H'-grade mean better job prospects.

Here are some of the less traditionally female jobs that may appeal to you.

Air Traffic Control Officer:

Controls aircraft flights in the United Kingdom, using radar and radio to tell pilots their position and keep planes a safe distance apart. At least two 'A'-levels/three 'H'-grade passes including maths, a science and/or geography. Above all, must have an unflappable personality that can deal with a lot of stress.

Town Planner:

Plans for the use of land for housing, shops, industry, etc. Usually works for a local authority. Minimum two 'A'-levels/three 'H'-grades. Necessary subjects — English, maths and either geography, history or a foreign language. Must have a creative, but practical eye.

Jockey:

Maximum weight seven stones for flat racing, ten stones for national hunt. No qualifications required for entry to training, but they are an advantage. Obviously, a love of horses is a must.

Obviously, with thousands of jobs to choose from, we can't tell you all of them — the ones we've looked at, though, might let you know that there are an awful lot of choices for you when you're thinking about your subjects, or deciding what you want to do with the qualifications you have.

The most important thing after all this, however, is that you go and talk to the careers officer at your school, or go to your local careers office (the number will be in the phone book). They'll be able to give you the answers to any questions you may have about your future. However, don't imagine that he or she will suddenly open your eyes to a brand new future — they can only guide you — in the end, it's going to be all up to you! Good luck!

Check out a copy of the Radio 1 "Options '88" Book for more information.

SCHOOLGIRL TRANSFORMED!

Stylist, Sharz, from Rainbow Room Education, Glasgow, begins the transformation.

Looking less bumpkinish by the minute . . .!

As make-up is applied, the siren begins to emerge!

The transformation is complete! No wonder her friends are jealous!

PATCHES WORKS THAT GOOD OLD MAKEOVER MAGIC YET AGAIN!

Teenagers all over the country were still reeling from shock last night after seeing Catie Muirhead transformed from schoolgirl to siren in a Patches makeover.

Pretty Miss Muirhead (15) said, "I wrote to Patches because I was fed up of my school mates calling me a country bumpkin just because I live in the middle of nowhere and have rosy cheeks. Now, of course, they're all jealous of me."

Take a look at our exclusive pictures to find out what all the fuss is about.

Hair by Rainbow Room Education, Royal Exchange Square, Glasgow.

Catie, the shy schoolgirl.

LOVE IS...

The Chambers 20th Century Dictionary describes love as being, "fondness: charity: an affection of the mind: strong liking" but it's been described in a number of weird and wonderful ways. We found out what a few famous celebs thought about love and romance and slushy stuff like that . . .

❚❚ I'm not one for candle-lit dinners. My romantic side is a private part of me which doesn't come out when I'm meeting people to do with my job.❚❚

Rick Astley

❚❚ I will never have a relationship in my life.❚❚

Morrissey

❚❚ My girlfriend threw me out. You've got to divide up all your stuff. Who gets the Sigue Sigue Sputnik record? I lost. I had to keep it!❚❚

Ben Elton

❚❚ I think it'll happen one day when I'm not thinking about it. I believe in love at first sight and I think I'll just know. Within an hour I'll know!❚❚

Matt Goss

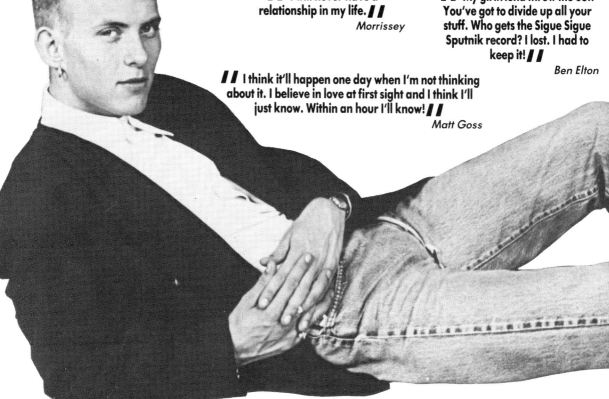

|| I find it takes me a long time to fall in love with a girl. I used to be able to say, 'I love you' very easily, but I realise now that it's not something you should say too lightly, or too quickly. It takes time to fall in love. ||

Jon Cryer

|| Women instinctively know what a *real* stud is. 39% of women think that a man's sexiest attribute is a small firm bottom. But look here — we're talking minorities. What about the other 61%, they're the ones I'm interested in! ||

Robbie Coltrane

|| I don't want a steady girlfriend to get in the way of where I'm going right now. But I'm romantic enough to say that could change in a day. ||

Matt Dillon

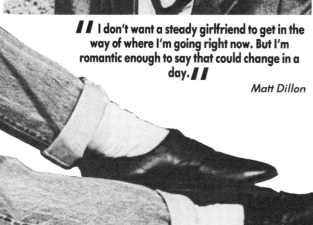

Now you know what other people think about romance and smoochy stuff, but what about you? What do you find romantic and, more to the point, what's a real turn-off?

If you haven't a clue, we've got the lowdown on romantic situations, presents and songs (and their yukky opposites):

The things that dreams are made of :

Walks along the beach at dusk.
Walking in the country on a summer's day.
Phone-calls just to say 'hello'.
Candle-lit dinners for two.
A night curled up together watching an old weepy on TV.
Listening to a song because it reminds you of the first time you met.
Trust.

Nightmare time :

Watching the latest "Rambo" video while he jumps up and down shouting, "Get 'im, Ramb!"
Walking through the city centre on a Saturday — even he can't take your mind off of the screaming kids and vicious shoppers!
Jealousy.
Going to a football match with him and seeing him at his worst, shouting abuse and then going in a huff when his team loses.

Smoochy Songs :

Diana Ross and Lionel Richie: "Endless Love".
The Commodores: "Three Times A Lady".
The Police: "Every Breath You Take".
Stevie Wonder: "I Just Called To Say I Love You".
Chris De Burgh: "Lady In Red".
Eddie Cochran: "Three Steps To Heaven".

Songs to kill the moment:

Elvis Presley: "Return To Sender".
The Rolling Stones: "(I Can't Get No) Satisfaction".
Benny Hill: "Ernie (The Fastest Milkman In The West)".
St. Winifred's School Choir: "There's No-One Quite Like Grandma".
Spitting Image: "The Chicken Song".
Michael Jackson: "Billie Jean".

Presents to touch your heart (aww!):

Heart-shaped chocolates (well, *any* chocolates).
Flowers — especially red roses.
Perfume.

Presents to make you wonder if romance is actually dead:

Oven gloves.
The full range of acne treatment products.
A pink quilted neck-to-toe housecoat.

Now you've seen what is and isn't romantic, you'll be able to recognise the sentimental slop when you see it. What about love? Well, you'll know it when it hits you!!

Two's Company...

Sharon and Lucy had known each other for years. They did nearly everything together . . .

IT'S A SHAME YOU DIDN'T GET TO THE DISCO ON SATURDAY, LUCY. YOU'LL NEVER GUESS WHO WAS THERE.

BETTER THAN THAT. IAIN LAWSON.

MY UNCLE WAS VISITING US AND MUM SAID IT WOULD LOOK RUDE IF I WENT OUT. SO, WHO'D I MISS? JASON DONOVAN?

HE WALKED ME HOME AFTER THE DISCO, AND I WENT ROLLER-SKATING WITH HIM YESTERDAY.

OH . . . I WAS WONDERING WHY YOU NEVER CAME ROUND . . .

ARE YOU GOING OUT WITH HIM AGAIN?

YEAH, HE'S SMASHING. I STILL CAN'T BELIEVE MY LUCK!

WHAT'D I SAY WRONG? SHE LOOKS LIKE SOMEBODY JUST DIED!

SHARON ISN'T THE ONLY ONE WHO THINKS IAIN'S SMASHING. I'VE FANCIED HIM FOR AGES. I THOUGHT SHE KNEW THAT.

STILL, I CAN'T BLAME SHARON FOR GOING OUT WITH HIM IF HE ASKED HER. I'D BETTER NOT LET HER KNOW HOW JEALOUS I FEEL. IT WOULD BE DAFT IF WE FELL OUT OVER SOMETHING LIKE THIS.

After school . . .

I WISH SHARON WOULDN'T KEEP GOING ON ABOUT IAIN. SHE HASN'T TALKED ABOUT ANYTHING ELSE SINCE WE SAT DOWN.

. . . AND HE ISN'T JUST A HUNK TO LOOK AT, HE'S GOT A TERRIFIC SENSE OF HUMOUR AS WELL . . .

HE SHOULD BE HERE IN ABOUT TEN MINUTES, ACTUALLY.

YOU MEAN IAIN'S MEETING YOU HERE? WHY'D YOU DRAG ME ALONG WITH YOU, THEN?

IT WASN'T WORTH GOING HOME FROM SCHOOL FIRST AND I DIDN'T WANT TO SIT ABOUT WAITING ON MY OWN. YOU DON'T MIND KEEPING ME COMPANY TILL HE GETS HERE, DO YOU?

And . . .

HI, SHARON, SORRY I'M LATE. OH . . . HELLO, LUCY. I DIDN'T KNOW YOU'D BOTH BE HERE.

IT'S OK, IAIN, I'M GOING IN A MINUTE. I WAS JUST KEEPING SHARON COMPANY.

DON'T BE DAFT. HANG ON AND HAVE A COFFEE WITH US.

I FEEL A BIT OF A GOOSEBERRY SITTING HERE WITH THEM, BUT I SUPPOSE IT'S BETTER THAN BEING ON MY OWN. THEY DON'T SEEM TO MIND, ANYWAY.

I THOUGHT LUCY WOULD LEAVE WHEN IAIN GOT HERE. I CAN'T TALK TO HIM PROPERLY WITH HER SITTING NEXT TO US!

Afterwards . . .

SEE YOU AT THE DISCO AS USUAL ON WEDNESDAY NIGHT?

OK. BUT . . . DIDN'T I HEAR IAIN SAYING HE'D BE THERE? YOU TWO WON'T WANT ME HANGING AROUND AGAIN, WILL YOU?

WHY NOT? WE'VE ALWAYS GONE TO THE DISCO TOGETHER ON WEDNESDAY. IT DOESN'T HAVE TO CHANGE JUST 'COS I'VE GOT A BOYFRIEND NOW.

THAT'S NICE OF SHARON. SHE'S DOING HER BEST TO MAKE SURE I DON'T FEEL LEFT OUT, NOW THAT SHE'S GOING WITH IAIN.

IAIN SAID HE MIGHT HAVE TO LEAVE EARLY ON WEDNESDAY NIGHT, AND I HATE WALKING HOME ON MY OWN. IT'LL BE HANDY TO HAVE LUCY THERE FOR COMPANY, JUST IN CASE!

And . . .

NO, 'COURSE I DON'T MIND LUCY BEING WITH US TONIGHT. I KNOW WHAT GOOD PALS YOU TWO ARE. WHY DON'T YOU BRING HER TO DANNY'S PARTY ON SATURDAY AS WELL? SHE'D PROBABLY ENJOY IT.

WELL . . . IF YOU REALLY THINK SO . . .

I WAS HOPING I'D HAVE IAIN TO MYSELF ON SATURDAY NIGHT!

IT WAS NICE OF SHARON TO INVITE ME TO THAT PARTY WITH THEM AT THE WEEKEND. I'M REALLY LUCKY TO HAVE SUCH A CONSIDERATE FRIEND.

I COULDN'T DO ANYTHING ELSE AFTER IAIN SUGGESTED IT. I JUST HOPE IT'S NOT GOING TO GET TO BE A HABIT!

But, several weeks later . . .

I JUST WANTED HER ALONG FOR COMPANY AT THE START, WHEN I WASN'T SURE IF IAIN WOULD BE THERE. I DIDN'T KNOW IT WOULD BECOME A PERMANENT THING! I'LL NEED TO THINK OF SOMETHING . . .

So . . .

YOU'VE FIXED ME UP WITH A DATE FOR SATURDAY NIGHT? WHAT DO YOU MEAN?

A FOURSOME. IAIN'S BRINGING HIS COUSIN, STEVE, AND HE SAYS HE'S NICE. YOU'LL LIKE HIM.

On Saturday night . . .

HI, GIRLS. MEET STEVE. HE'S JUST MOVED HERE FROM MANCHESTER.

WOW . . . HE'S GORGEOUS!

HE DOESN'T LOOK VERY INTERESTED IN ME. IF ANYTHING, HE SEEMS KEENER ON SHARON!

Continued on page 25. 15

HOW TO GET NOTICED BY THE MAN OF YOUR DREAMS

(IF ALL ELSE FAILS!).

How often has it happened? You've put on a full face of perfect make-up, your hair's in place, and you've got all your latest "Next" gear on and he *still* hasn't batted an eyelash in your direction! Well, take heart, 'cos Patches'll save the day! Read on . . .

1. Stuff your face with loads of calorie-ridden foods — I mean, who can fail to notice an eighteen stone lump . . .?

2. Let your new "Scarlet Dream" lipstick smudge all over your teeth — then smile, of course . . .

3. Wear white high heels with fake tan (showing the finger streaks) or, even better, wear American Tan tights . . .

4. Always, *always* put your blusher on as two thick, red streaks. If he doesn't see *you*, he'll definitely notice a clown . . .

5. Go home and pig out on Monster Munches, a fish supper (or two), Dairy Milk bars, hot chocolate and a mega-McDonalds. Didn't he say he loved cheese and tomato pizza? Well, he'll love your face then . . .

6. Go for a strenuous game of hockey in P.E. — but don't shower afterwards or wear deodorant. Then you can seductively sway past him in the canteen and watch him drop his tray at the dreadful "aroma" that has hit him . . .

7. Dress up as a gorilla-gram and make your unexpected entrance at the local disco. He couldn't possibly ignore an amorous gorilla, could he . . .?

8. Take a sudden "fainting spell" and collapse across his desk in maths. Wrapping your arms around his neck at the same time . . .

9. Model yourself on your all-time hero; the jokes, humour, style of dressing, perfume, etc. Who? Robbie Coltrane, of course . . .

10. Forget to shave your legs . . . for over a year. You never know, he might go for a girl who has legs like an orang-utang . . .

Well, now that you've giggled your way through the list, try to forget every single one of them 'cos we were only joking — honestly!

ALL AROUND THE WORLD!

WHETHER YOU FANCY YOURSELF AS A SULTRY SENORITA

OR AN AMERICAN TEEN-QUEEN, STYLE PROVIDES

THE LOW DOWN ON THE FASHION AND BEAUTY LOOKS THAT COUNT.

FRENCH

THE original French style is still a favourite: pencil skirts and Bardot tops. A narrow silhouette demands fabrics that stretch and cling, while stripes are a must for off-the-shoulder tops. Lacy tights, high heels, wide belts and, of course, the beret, all add up to this sophisticated image. Only for the figure-conscious and ultra-confident — could you be a sexy mademoiselle?!

FRENCH women are famous for their sexy pouts, so the most important cosmetic for this look is a bright red lipstick — and we mean bright!

Outline with a red lip-pencil (just outside your natural lip-line if you feel your lips are a little too thin), then fill in with lashings of scarlet lipstick.

A beige foundation and some tawny blusher just under the cheekbones gives a dramatic shape to the face, while a mixture of browns and pinks on the eyelids gives warmth and definition without looking too heavy.

Add the finishing touches with a touch of dark brown eyeliner and some mascara.

SPANISH

CREATE the Spanish/Mexican look with full, tiered skirts, petticoats, boleros and waistcoats. Black and white are best, with touches of scarlet. Suede meets cotton, and embroidery can be glimpsed on anything and everything. Large hooped earrings and a flat-topped hat are the finishing touches. Ideally a summer look, go for the señorita style, and sizzle in the sun.

SPANISH women love make-up and like it to be obvious!

Choose a medium foundation or a translucent bronzing gel, especially if you've still got the remnant of a tan.

Eyes are dark and sultry — we used two shades of grey and plenty of black eyeliner. Remember to darken your eyebrows with a black eyebrow pencil, squaring off the ends to give a more definite shape.

Lips are red and glossy — choose a moisturised lipstick or some clear gloss brushed over the top.

AMERICAN

STYLE goes down on the range for the cowgirl look. Denim is essential, whether it's jeans or a mini; and any shirt with fringes looks good on top. Fabrics are hard-wearing and natural and most colours will do. Leather cowboy boots and belts are necessary accessories, and a neckerchief and hat are the icing on the cake. For a wholesome style, go for this all-American look, and get right on down to the ranch!

THE Western American girls pride themselves on their healthy complexions, so choose a light liquid foundation and cover any spots or blemishes with a concealer stick.

Define eyes with earthy shades of gold and brown well-blended to get rid of harsh lines. Mascara should be brown — black is too harsh — and both blusher and lipstick should be natural tawny or peach shades.

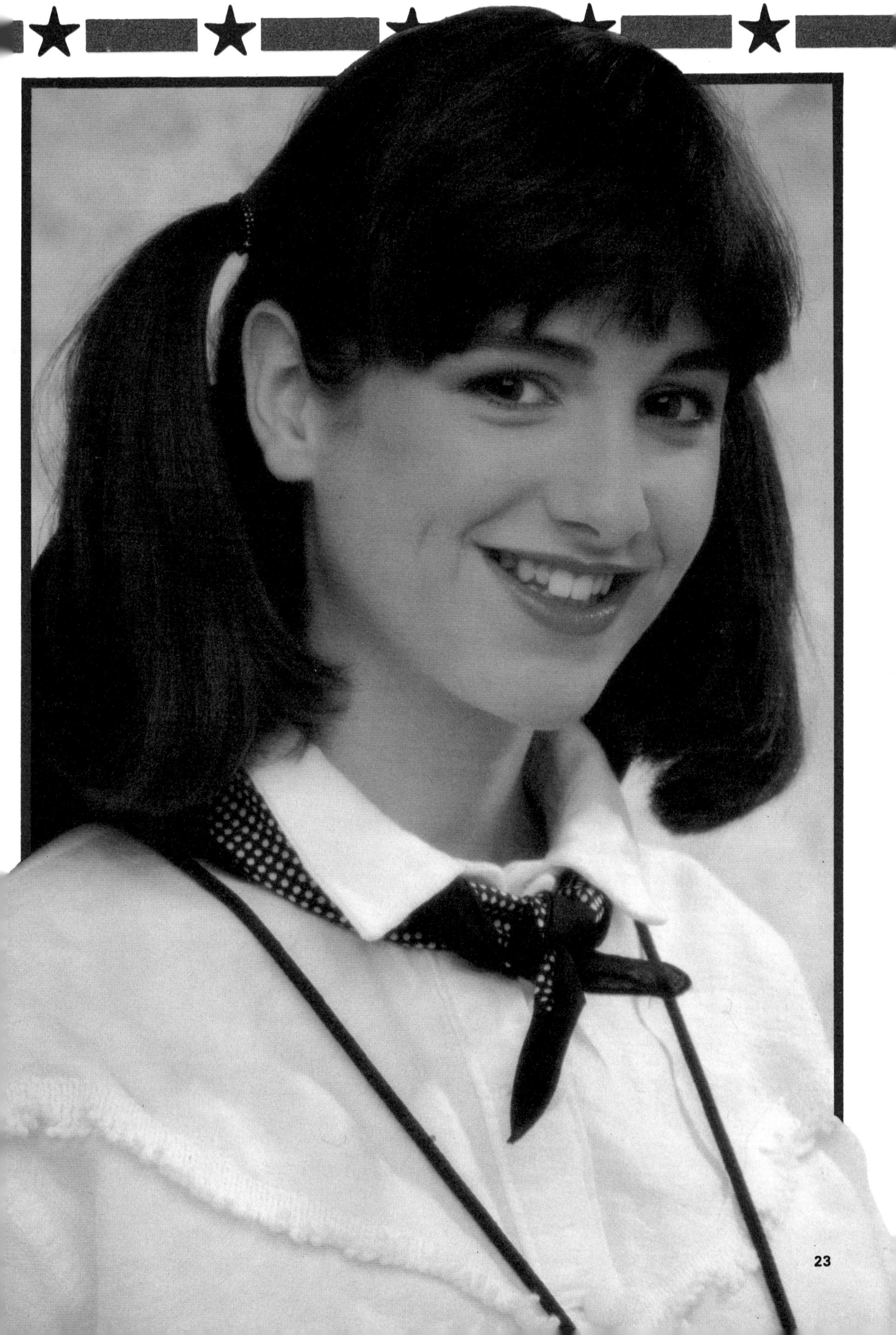

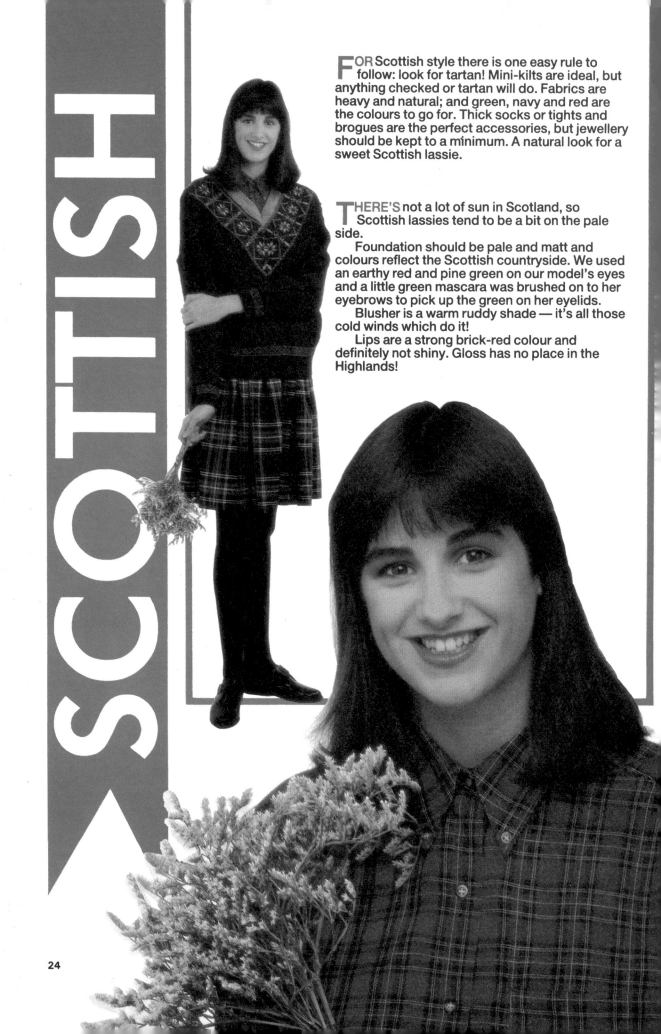

SCOTTISH

FOR Scottish style there is one easy rule to follow: look for tartan! Mini-kilts are ideal, but anything checked or tartan will do. Fabrics are heavy and natural; and green, navy and red are the colours to go for. Thick socks or tights and brogues are the perfect accessories, but jewellery should be kept to a minimum. A natural look for a sweet Scottish lassie.

THERE'S not a lot of sun in Scotland, so Scottish lassies tend to be a bit on the pale side.

Foundation should be pale and matt and colours reflect the Scottish countryside. We used an earthy red and pine green on our model's eyes and a little green mascara was brushed on to her eyebrows to pick up the green on her eyelids.

Blusher is a warm ruddy shade — it's all those cold winds which do it!

Lips are a strong brick-red colour and definitely not shiny. Gloss has no place in the Highlands!

THIS IS TERRIBLE. I'M DOING MY BEST TO MAKE CONVERSATION, BUT STEVE'S HARDLY LISTENING. I DON'T THINK HE'S MY TYPE, ANYWAY.

IT'S A PITY IAIN'S HERE. I WOULDN'T MIND GETTING TO KNOW HIS COUSIN A BIT BETTER!

Afterwards . . .

IT WAS NICE OF YOU TO TRY AND FIND ME A BOYFRIEND, SHARON, BUT STEVE COULDN'T EVEN REMEMBER MY NAME WHEN WE WERE SAYING GOODNIGHT!

NO WONDER. YOU JUST SAT THERE LIKE A FROZEN FISH ALL NIGHT. AT THIS RATE, IAIN AND I WILL BE STUCK WITH YOU ALL THE TIME!

OK, IF THAT'S HOW YOU FEEL, DON'T WORRY. I WON'T BE A NUISANCE TO YOU AND IAIN ANY MORE . . .

NOW HER FEELINGS ARE HURT. WELL, I CAN'T HELP THAT. IT'S NOT MY FAULT, IS IT?

At school on Monday . . .

I REALLY THOUGHT SHARON WAS MY BEST PAL. BUT I CAN'T BLAME HER FOR FEELING THE WAY SHE DOES.

But after school . . .

HI. NOT GOT YOUR PAL WITH YOU TODAY?

NO . . . EM . . . WE DON'T REALLY HANG ABOUT TOGETHER ALL THAT MUCH.

I THOUGHT HE WAS GORGEOUS WHEN IAIN BROUGHT HIM ALONG ON SATURDAY — HE LOOKS EVEN BETTER TODAY!

I'M SORRY ABOUT SATURDAY NIGHT. IT WAS A BIT OF A DISASTER, WASN'T IT?

IT WAS JUST THAT I DIDN'T HAVE MUCH IN COMMON WITH YOUR PAL. WHEN I SAW THE TWO OF YOU, I WAS HOPING SHE WAS IAIN'S GIRLFRIEND AND YOU WERE GOING TO BE MINE!

ARE YOU SEEING IAIN TONIGHT?

I'M SUPPOSED TO BE. BUT I COULD ALWAYS CHANGE MY MIND IF I GOT A BETTER OFFER!

Later . . .

OH, THERE'S SHARON AND IAIN'S COUSIN IN THE QUEUE FOR THE PICTURES. IAIN MUST BE MEETING THEM HERE.

Continued on page 28 25

HOLDING BACK THE YEARS . . .

COME with us — put on your skin-tight jeans, your biggest plastic earrings and massive sweater and let's take a walk back through time. To begin with, back to your local High Street in the mid-sixties . . .

9 a.m. on a sunny, summer Saturday and the street's buzzing. Let's go and have a look. Be careful crossing, as there are no Pelican crossings — go down to the lights — wait — OK. Now.

You must have noticed how short the skirts are. You wonder why some of the girls bother to wear one at all! Their shoes are pretty, though, aren't they? Delicate, round-toed slippers, with sling-backs and tiny square heels. What's really throwing you is the hairstyles. You've seen pictures, of course, but to actually see it! It's almost sinister, and very, well — sixties! Look at those two girls giggling over the hat counter. The make-up! Huge, black panda eyes and pale lipstick. Wonder what they're laughing at. Let's listen . . .

"... mmm, that's nice."

"Yeah, what d'you think of this one?"

"Yuk! You look like my gran on the way to the bingo."

"This one, then."

"Ooooh, that's lovely!"

"Mmm, s'pose so."

"Anyway, listen. What say we go down to Revolvers and listen to the new Beatles record?"

"Yeah, OK. But I heard it on 'Ready, Steady, Go!' last week — didn't like it."

"You never like them at first, but I think it'll grow on you. Come on."

Let's follow them. There they are, talking to the boy serving in Revolvers . . .

"... you do, do you? What's it worth? Last dance tonight?"

"Not likely, Pete Jackson. Not if you were the last man on earth. Anyway, you know I can never stay till the end. I've got to be in by eleven — Dad'll kill me if I'm not!"

"Aww, come on!"

"Go on, Liz. I'm dying to hear the record again!"

"Oh, all right. But put the flaming record on quickly!"

Suddenly the shop is filled with the sound of the Beatles . . . crowded in here, isn't it? Let's go somewhere else and have a coffee. There's a Kardomah just around the corner and they always have lovely cakes . . .

There you are. Vanilla Slice. OK? See that girl behind the counter? Probably still at school. This'll be a Saturday job. Anyone

Wherever you're reading this Patches Annual — in front of the box, in your room (what about that homework?!) — stop for a moment . . . and think about your mum. Who is she, really? She's not just your mum, you know. She is a person in her own right and was once the same age as you. Sometime during the sixties or fifties she wanted things like you, moaned over her homework like you and agonised over boys . . . just like you.

who wanted a Saturday job — or any other sort of job come to that — could get one. No problem. There was something in the air then. I think it was confidence. A confident hope that, as Bob Dylan said, "the times they are a-changin'" and it was going to be for the better!

Discos started in the sixties, you know, only they were called discotheques then. After she's finished work on Saturday, the sixties girl would dash home, bathe, change and be out to the discotheque before you could say Rolling Stones. She was very sophisticated, or thought she was — she'd rather have a Chinese or an Indian than steak and chips any day, though she'd happily ram down a Wimpy before spending the rest of her lunch hour shopping. The sixties girl had money in her pocket, and she meant to enjoy it. The feminist movement was just a speck on the distant horizon, and marriage and babies still beckoned — but not yet. That was the future and, in the meantime, she was going to have fun. After all, who knew what might happen tomorrow?

WELL, OK. Finished your cake? Let's go a bit further this time . . . back in time. Wrap your big sweater round you and hold tight . . . back another ten years to your High Street in the mid-fifties . . .

9 a.m. again. Sunny again, only this time there's a difference. Can you hear it? There are plenty of buses and some taxis, but not many cars, compared to what you're used to. In the fifties, most ordinary people like you and me didn't have cars. The buses were cheap, reliable and frequent.

Hey, look at Revolvers, the record shop. It's an electrical shop now. There are three televisions in the window — huge things with a tiny screen at the top and a loudspeaker at the bottom. If our fifties girl had one at home, which wasn't very likely since not many people did, it would probably have been bought by her parents in 1953, so they could all sit and watch Queen Elizabeth's coronation "as it happened".

There are some portable radios on a shelf at the side of the window. Square and brown, ugly-looking things. At the back of the shop there are racks and racks of records — wait, though. C & A have opened. Let's look in . . .

Busy again. Just look at the blouses on that rack! They're

hideous! Purple things with massive buttons — ugh! Mind you, these aren't bad . . . white with tiny black studs and a velvet shoestring tie at the neck. M'mm. 5/11d. That's about 29p. TWENTY NINE PENCE? I'll have three! Wait a minute, I've only got ten and ninepence, which is about 54p in today's money. Now, if you were really here you'd need 3d for your bus home, 6d for your Youth Club fees tonight. If you wanted a coke, that'd take care of another 3d plus 1½d for a bag of crisps. Another 1/6 if you wanted to go to the pictures on Sunday night and . . . all right, all right — you've got the message!

Look at that skirt. It's brilliant! Dead straight, with a slit at the back. That girl's looking at it — she's going to buy it — shall we follow her for a bit?

She's going into the chemist, picked something up, can't quite see . . .

"Is this stuff any good?"

"It's smashing, love. I'm wearing it myself. Gives you a flawless complexion."

The girl behind the counter looks as though she's put a smooth, pale mask over her face, unshaded and unblushered, it looks flat and featureless.

The girl pads on another layer of mask. Our girl is looking at her critically.

"Yeah, I like it. Have you got a darker one?"

"Sure, we've got all sorts!"

"Thanks. Oh, and I want a Revlon lipstick, please. A red one."

The shop girl selects the lipstick and twirls it up. It's bright red, like blood.

"OK?"

"Yeah, and a pair of stockings, please. 15 denier, size 7, tan."

No such things as one size tights in those days, and don't let anyone tell you that suspenders are sexy. There's only one thing that suspenders are, and that's incredibly uncomfortable! Ask your mum.

She's heading for the bus station . . . going home. Wonder how far she's going? Listen a minute . . .

"Penny halfpenny, please."

M'mm, not far. Anyway, there's plenty to see. Look, tennis courts. Fancy playing tennis in a skirt that long! And look at the man's shorts! Longs, more like! There's a cinema — wonder what's on — Elvis Presley in "Love Me Tender" and coming soon, Marilyn Monroe in "Gentlemen Prefer Blondes" — good film that. Quick, she's

getting off . . .

As we can do anything we like in our time bubble, let's skip forward a few hours to 7 p.m. Time for our girl to go down to the Youth Club, via a trip to the coffee bar. She's scraped her hair back in a tight ponytail and put on huge hoop earrings. She's wearing the new black skirt and a tight black sweater, plus a three inch wide, black patent belt which pinches her waist.

She hesitated over high heels and nylons, or flat loafers and ankle socks, finally settling for the flats and socks, because she saw Debbie Reynolds wear them with a tight skirt in that film last week, and she looked great. A scarf tied cowboy fashion round her throat, a dab of that foundation, mascara and a bright red lipstick and she's ready!

The rest of the group are already at the coffee bar when she arrives. Her boyfriend makes a grab for her, then kisses her and goes off to get the coffee.

When he comes back, they're all arguing . . .

"Little Richard's a million miles better than Elvis. Any day."

"Anyway, what about Chuck Berry? If anyone really rocks, it's him."

"You've gotta be joking! "

And on they argue.

Later, at the club, an Elvis record is on the record player and, as they would have said themselves, the joint was really rockin'. Girls and boys are jiving madly in a haze of whirling skirts and petticoats, shoestring ties and drainpipe jeans, and huge oversized sweaters called Sloppy Joes. Towards the end of the evening, someone puts a Guy Mitchell record on, turns the lights down and, apart from the soft, plaintive voice on the record player and the shuffling of feet in a slow dance, there's nothing but silence . . . until the club closes and they all dash noisily down to the local chip shop for a threepenny bag of chips, and then her boyfriend will walk our fifties girl home . . .

In bed, maybe she'll remember a girl she saw in the High Street that morning. A pretty girl wearing drainpipe jeans, huge plastic earrings, a collared T-shirt and a Sloppy Joe. She won't remember her because of the odd clothes, because they weren't odd. Everybody wore things like that in the fifties. It was something else, something familiar, somehow. She only caught a glimpse of her, but she looked nice . . . bright . . . hopeful . . . If ever our fifties girl had a daughter, she'd like her to be like that . . .

But, moments later . . .

HI, IAIN. YOU'D BETTER HURRY UP IF YOU DON'T WANT TO MISS THE START OF THE FILM. SHARON AND STEVE ARE KEEPING YOUR PLACE IN THE QUEUE.

EH? SHARON'S WITH STEVE?

WHAT'S UP? DID I SAY SOMETHING WRONG?

I'M NOT SURE. SHARON PHONED AN HOUR AGO TO TELL ME SHE COULDN'T SEE ME . . .. 'COS SHE'D DECIDED TO STAY IN AND HAVE AN EARLY NIGHT!

Next day, there were two phone calls. First, Steve phoned Sharon . . .

YEAH, I ENJOYED MYSELF LAST NIGHT TOO, SHARON, BUT I DON'T THINK WE SHOULD SEE EACH OTHER AGAIN. I'D FEEL ROTTEN GOING OUT WITH YOU BEHIND IAIN'S BACK, ANYWAY.

So . . .

HI, IAIN. WHAT TIME'LL I SEE YOU TONIGHT?

YOU MUST BE JOKING! I HEARD ABOUT YOU GETTING OFF WITH STEVE LAST NIGHT. THAT'S WHY ! YOU COULDN'T SEE ME, ISN'T IT? WE'RE FINISHED, SHARON. I DON'T WANT TO GO OUT WITH SOMEBODY I CAN'T TRUST!

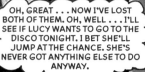

OH, GREAT . . . NOW I'VE LOST BOTH OF THEM. OH, WELL . . . I'LL SEE IF LUCY WANTS TO GO TO THE DISCO TONIGHT. I BET SHE'LL JUMP AT THE CHANCE. SHE'S NEVER GOT ANYTHING ELSE TO DO ANYWAY.

But . . .

SORRY, SHARON, I CAN'T. I'M GOING WITH SOMEBODY ELSE TONIGHT.

YOU ARE? WHO?

IAIN. HE SAID JUST 'COS HE'D SPLIT UP WITH YOU, THERE WAS NO REASON FOR HIM TO FALL OUT WITH ME AS WELL. WE'RE THINKING OF GOING TO THAT POP CONCERT TOMORROW, TOO.

I'D ASK YOU TO COME WITH US — BUT YOU KNOW WHAT THEY SAY ABOUT THREE BEING A CROWD . . .

THE END

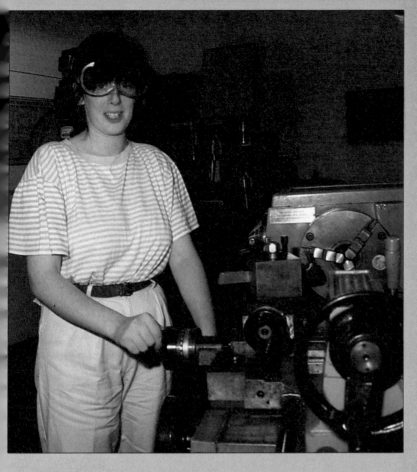

IT'S A MAN'S WORLD!

(OR IS IT . . . ?)

Have you ever considered taking up a career in a (so-called) man's job, then changed your mind, simply because you couldn't be bothered with the hassle you thought you'd encounter?

Well, Patches spoke to a few girls who'd decided to take the plunge, and ventured out into the fields of engineering, electronics and motor mechanics.

The girls we interviewed were still studying at college and we asked them a few questions about their trade and the various difficulties they'd had to face.

ENGINEERING

First on our hit list was Anne Smart (22), who was studying for an Ordinary National Certificate in Engineering. We interrupted her as she was fiddling around with a funny machine. "It's a lathe," she informed us. "It's for turning off metal." Anne works in a room full of boys, not surprisingly, and we asked her if she felt embarrassed when she first started. "Yes I did," she answers, laughing, "although, I think the boys felt just as awkward, having a girl in their class!"

At this point, Anne moved on to show us another machine. She seemed quite confident and at ease, and obviously enjoyed the work.

What made you decide to take up this line of work?

"Well, I had been a barmaid, office junior and kitchen assistant. There wasn't any thinking in it or any challenge. I wanted to make decisions for myself and this seemed the ideal job."

Being a girl, was it difficult for you to get on the course?

"No, actually, I was quite surprised because I wrote to the college, was given an interview shortly afterwards, and that was it! No-one seemed to have any reservations about taking a girl on the course."

Do you feel pressurised into doing better than boys, simply because you feel you have to prove yourself?

"Oh yes. I'm always studying, every night at home. The rest of the class have a bit of experience in this line of work, so I have to work a little bit harder to keep up with them."

Do you get any sort of harassment from classmates?

"Not really, no. The teachers are really polite, always telling the boys not to swear in front of me! Generally, though, they're pretty well behaved. I suppose they've just got used to me being in the class with them. They don't think about it any more."

How do you rate your chances of getting work when you leave the college course? Do you think people will be a bit doubtful about hiring a girl?

"Well, according to my lecturer, there's an awful high demand for engineers, so an employer shouldn't be too fussy if he's really needing a good engineer. I can't see any problem, personally."

Has there ever been a time when you've wished you'd taken a normal job, like typing?

"Not at all. I hate nine to five jobs — it's just something that I associate with boredom. I was always good at metalwork and woodwork at school, y'see. I enjoy working with my hands. I'd much rather be doing this, no matter what anyone says!"

ELECTRONIC SERVICING

We found these two girls studying wave frequencies on an electronic screen (Oscilloscope). These are the people you'll find coming to fix your TV in a few years time!

Karen Robertson (16) and Ellen

like my careers teacher! Other than that, they usually say, 'Well, that's a man's job, isn't it?', but I usually sort them out there!"

Ellen thinks that, in this job, a girl can do just as well as any man.

"So far, we haven't suffered any more difficulties than the boys on the course (they are the only girls in a group of ten boys). I think it's all a myth, this stuff about women not being as good at these jobs as men!"

Do you find you get let off with mistakes because you're a girl?

"No," says Karen. "If you make a mistake, they tell you. They don't treat us better or anything and if they find it necessary to shout at us, then they will!"

Why didn't you take a normal job, like a secretary or a hairdresser?

"Ha! I just **couldn't** do something like that! It's so **boring!** Nah, give me broken down TVs any day!"

Ellen's opinion was slightly different though. "Sometimes I wish I had taken a typing course, like the time when I was adjusting the line-synch in a TV and nearly blew myself up . . ."

Well, I think that's enough said there, folks. We'll leave them to it . . .

Croll (16) had only just left school but seemed to be very sure about what they were doing.

"I had an 'O' level in Physics, which is one qualification the college definitely wants you to have for this course," says Karen. "I had absolutely no doubt that this was the job I wanted to do. I didn't let anyone talk me out of it!"

What's the reaction you get from people, when you first tell them what you're studying?

"They laugh," says Ellen. "My dad thought it was really funny and he tried to change my mind about it,

MOTOR VEHICLE MECHANICS

Meet Eleanor Warren (19). She's the only girl in her class, but

nevertheless, she seemed quite happy amidst the stink of petrol and oil-stained overalls.

What made you take up this line of work?

"Well, it's something different and I genuinely like cars. I **couldn't** do anything else and I certainly wouldn't do an office job."

Why not?

"I can't sit down," she answered. "I'd hate all that having-to-smile-and-paint-your-nails business. Anyway, I like working with my hands — and boys," she added, as an afterthought. "I don't get on with girls, really."

What did your parents think of all this?

"Well, my dad was a bit surprised. I think he was hoping I'd go on to university like him — he's a lecturer, you see. However, he soon got used to the idea and my mum loved it! She was quite keen for me, too. She likes me to have a challenge."

Do you feel under pressure at all?

"I don't think I get the chance to prove myself, because I'm not allowed to do certain things. Like when I'm working on a car with a boy, they don't like me jacking the car up or anything. They just don't think I can do it."

Unlike the other girls, Eleanor was not embarrassed starting her course in a class of boys.

"No, I wasn't embarrassed at all. My best friends are boys and I get on well with them. I **never** feel awkward around boys."

Have you ever wished you hadn't taken the course?

"Yes, fairly recently, as a matter of fact. I was working on this car with a boy and he refused to let me do anything, and I got quite upset about it and wished I hadn't done the course. Then I thought, 'No, I'll show him I **can** do it!' so I kicked up a fuss and was allowed to work on my own car. I'm a very determined person in case you hadn't noticed!"

We reckoned she'd **have** to be determined, to do a job like that.

We watched her at work, as she continued telling us about the job. Spanner in hand, she said, "There's very little problem, in the physical aspect. I can lift an engine just as easily as a boy, in fact, I can do **anything** as good as a boy!"

We believe you, Eleanor, and good luck to all the other girls who want to have a career in these jobs!

Mike and Sara had decided to get engaged at Christmas . . .

ARE YOU SURE YOU DON'T MIND IT BEING A SECOND-HAND RING, LOVE? WE COULD STILL CHOOSE A NEW ONE FROM THE JEWELLER'S, IF YOU WANT.

NO, I THINK THIS ONE'S LOVELY, MIKE. THE DESIGN'S REALLY UNUSUAL.

IT WAS MY AUNT'S. IT'S BETTER THAN ANYTHING I COULD HAVE AFFORDED TO BUY FOR YOU, BUT I WASN'T SURE HOW YOU'D FEEL ABOUT WEARING A RING THAT USED TO BELONG TO SOMEBODY ELSE.

I LIKE IT, MIKE. IT'S NICE TO THINK YOU'VE GIVEN ME SOMETHING THAT'S BEEN IN YOUR FAMILY SO LONG. IT MAKES IT SEEM EVEN MORE SPECIAL.

RING OF EVIL

I'D BETTER GET BACK AND HELP MUM GET THINGS READY FOR TONIGHT. YOU WON'T BE LATE, WILL YOU?

FOR MY OWN ENGAGEMENT PARTY? I WOULDN'T DARE! SEE YOU THERE ABOUT 8 O'CLOCK, OK?

I CAN HARDLY BELIEVE MIKE AND I ARE REALLY ENGAGED. IT'S ALL HAPPENED SO FAST. FOUR MONTHS AGO WE DIDN'T EVEN KNOW EACH OTHER! NOW I JUST CAN'T IMAGINE LIFE WITHOUT HIM.

Sara's parents weren't quite so happy about the engagement . . .

IT'S NOT THAT WE'VE ANYTHING AGAINST MIKE, DEAR. WE JUST WISH WE KNEW A BIT MORE ABOUT HIM. WE'VE NEVER EVEN MET HIS FAMILY.

I TOLD YOU BEFORE, MUM, HE HASN'T GOT ANY. HIS PARENTS ARE DEAD AND HE WAS BROUGHT UP BY HIS AUNT. AFTER SHE DIED, HE MOVED HERE TO LOOK FOR A JOB AND THAT'S HOW HE FINISHED UP WORKING IN THE COFFEE BAR.

I KNOW YOU THINK WE'VE GOT ENGAGED TOO SOON, MUM, BUT MIKE'S REALLY SPECIAL. THERE'S NOTHING YOU CAN SAY THAT'LL CHANGE MY MIND ABOUT HIM.

WE KNOW THAT, SARA. THAT'S WHY WE HAVEN'T TRIED TO STOP YOU. YOU'D GO AHEAD ANYWAY, WHATEVER WE SAID. BUT JUST REMEMBER ONE THING; IF YOU EVER HAVE ANY DOUBTS ABOUT IT, IT'S NEVER TOO LATE TO CHANGE YOUR MIND.

At the engagement party . . .

YOUR RING'S LOVELY, SARA.

ISN'T IT? IT BELONGED TO MIKE'S AUNT.

CAN I SEE?

Continued on page 38

33

WHO'S THE MAN FOR YOU?

Wouldn't it be brilliant to be rich and famous? Imagine jet-setting around the world, staying in the best hotels, wearing great clothes — and best of all, mixing with all those famous hunky men!

But which is the right one for you? Would you make an ideal match for Marti Pellow, or are you exactly right for George Michael?

Read on and find out . . .

1) At long last, the man of your dreams has asked you out. How does he do it?

B — He turns up on your doorstep, gets down on bended knee and recites a love poem he wrote for you.

C — He telephones you, as he's a bit embarrassed to ask you in person.

A — He sends round an enormous bouquet of roses and lilies with a gilt-edged card, asking you for a date.

2) What time does he turn up for your date?

B — Almost an hour late. He saw some lovely bluebells in the park and just had to sit down and admire their beauty at leisure.

A — On time, of course.

C — Twenty minutes late — he was watching the big match on TV.

3) How does he arrive?

C — In his souped-up Capri with the subtle 'go-faster' stripes and halogen spotlights.

B — On foot or on his trusty bicycle — even if it's pouring with rain.

A — In a gleaming limo, driven by a uniformed chauffeur.

4) What's your date wearing?

C — Whatever he put on when he got up that morning — he's not a great believer in dressing up.

B — Something he found in an antique or secondhand shop, and altered himself.

A — Designer jeans, sunglasses and a leather jacket which cost him six weeks' wages.

5) What are his first words to you?

A — "You look gorgeous, darling. Love your dress."

B — "You look lovely. I've never noticed how blue your eyes are before."

C — "Er . . . hi! Are you . . . er . . . ready, then?"

6) So where do you go together?

C — Well, first it's to the local flea-pit to see Rambo III, followed by a pizza in a fast food bar and a long, romantic walk home.

A — A trip to the cinema to see a sub-titled Italian film (first prizewinner at the Latvian Arts Festival), followed by a meal in a Japanese restaurant and a romantic stroll along the riverbank.

B — A trip to the opening of his friend's photography exhibition, then a quiet meal to discuss the deeper meaning of some of the photos.

7) How does he act during the evening?

A — Very gentlemanly and sophisticated, always making sure you're comfortable and having a good time.

C — He's a bit shy at first but soon becomes jokey and amusing, keeping you in fits of giggles most of the time.

B — He's very caring and spends lots of time staring into your eyes and telling you what a lovely person you are.

8) And, at the end of the evening, how does he say goodbye?

B — He strokes your hand while he tells you what a wonderful time he's had, then kisses you gently on the cheek.

A — He hands you a single red rose, then gives you a lovely soft kiss which leaves you with your knees knocking as he strolls down the path to his car.

C — He shuffles around for about ten minutes on your doorstep, then just as you think you're about to fall asleep, he lunges at you, misses his aim and kisses the wall behind you.

MAINLY A's

Well, there's no doubt about it — you are a pretty sophisticated lady. You want to be wined and dined by candlelight, pampered with gifts and compliments and treated with a bit of respect.

And who better to give you a taste of high-class living than superstar George Michael?

Smooth, suave and sophisticated, he'd never let you down or embarrass you — all in all, a perfect gentleman for the perfect lady!

MAINLY B's

Let's face it, you're a bit of a dreamer. You'd love to go back to the days of long skirts and flouncy petticoats, when ladies simpered behind gloved hands.

You love the beauties of nature and all kinds of art, and nothing fills you with more emotion than a Victorian love sonnet or a beautiful painting.

Your ideal man just has to be Lloyd Cole — sensitive and thoughtful, someone who appreciates that the best things in life are often free!

MAINLY C's

As someone who's practical and down-to-earth, you want a guy who says what he thinks, does what he wants and doesn't spend time day-dreaming.

Marti Pellow from Wet Wet Wet is your kind of man. With his sense of humour, he'll keep you amused for hours on end and cheer you up when you're feeling depressed.

A likeable chap, your mum would love to have him round for tea and your dad would quite happily take him for a game of snooker!

HAPPY EVER AFTER?

ROSAMUND AND MAGWITCH WERE SISTERS — BUT YOU'D NEVER KNOW IT. ROSAMUND WAS BEAUTIFUL AND WICKED WHEREAS MAGWITCH WAS ANGELIC BUT UGLY. WOULD THE HANDSOME, DASHING PRINCE FALL FOR ROSAMUND OR WOULD HE SEE THE INNER BEAUTY OF MAGWITCH . . . ?

ONCE upon a time, long ago and in a country far away, there lived two princesses.

Now one of them, Rosamund, was the 22-carat-genuine story-book type: long, golden hair, sapphire-blue eyes, ruby-red lips, millions in the bank, etc., etc., whereas the other, Magwitch, was as ugly as her sister was beautiful and broke, to boot. Magwitch had thin, black, greasy hair which clung to her head in strands, a squint, and a long pointed nose which dripped a lot. She was broke because she gave away every penny she could get her hands on to the 'deserving poor', while Rosamund salted away every penny in the bank, where it would earn interest and make her even richer.

In other words, Rosamund was beautiful, rich and a nasty piece of work, whereas Magwith was ugly, poor, and a saint.

Well now, one fine winter's morning, who should ride into the kingdom but a handsome prince looking for a wife.

"Yo, minion," he yelled to a peasant who'd just popped out of his humble hovel to see if there were any princes riding by.

"Yo there! I am on a quest and require your assistance, scumbag!" he shouted again, and the peasant staggered back, barefoot in the snow, wringing his hands in horror.

"Oh no — not a quest to slay the dragon of Ruralbania and in doing so win the hand of the Princess Rosamund, oh wonderful sire!" he said in a peasantish voice.

"Er — no," said the prince, looking suddenly uncomfortable. "There's always a catch, isn't there? Can't I just marry the princess without all this slaying palaver?"

"Oh, I should think so," said the peasant, humbly and getting colder by the millisecond. "You could always ask, couldn't you? After all, if you ask me — which you didn't, but I'll tell you anyway — if you ask me, all this dragon-slaying . . . well, I mean, it's just tradition, innit? Anyway, what use is it, that's what I'd like to know, dead princes cluttering the kingdom up . . ."

"Thank you, serf," said the prince. "Now if you'd just direct me to the palace?"

"Straight down yonder dirt track for half a mile, left at the forest, first on the right and you'll find the palace half way up the mountain. Can't miss it. It's the only one with golden turrets . . ." At this, he stopped as the grovelling had made him feel quite giddy.

"Thank you, minion — I shall see that your hovel isn't burned down this Christmas," said the prince, and galloped off down the path.

Arriving at the palace gates, he reined in his black charger, leaped athletically from the saddle, caught his foot in the stirrup and landed flat on his face in the crisp white snow.

As he vainly attempted to cover up the huge dent in the snow, and brush it from his tunic, a palace sentry, who'd been guarding the gate since dawn that morning and was cold and bad-tempered, mumbled, "Wally."

"Do you mind!" said the prince, wincing as the snow fell into his boot, melted and seeped into the socks his mummy had knitted him. "I am a prince."

"Quite," said the sentry. He'd seen them all and he just couldn't be bothered being nice to this drongo.

"And I wish to see your master, the king."

"Zat right?"

"Yes."

"Tough."

"Isn't he in?"

The sentry picked some snow from his uniform, smoothed it on his hair, combed a new parting — the last one had disappeared in a snow storm — then said, menacingly, "Maybe he is . . . maybe he isn't . . . it depends how much it's worth."

"Oh, I forgot . . . just a moment," the prince said, feeling slightly embarrassed — he had been told of the servants in these parts demanding tips but in the heat, well, the freezing cold, of the moment, he'd forgotten.

He scrabbled in his pocket and brought out four brass buttons (which had fallen off his tunic at various times), two pieces of string (string's always useful), a fragment of chalk (for leaving messages on trees), a bus pass, a handkerchief, three balls of fluff, a Matchbox dumper truck and a white rat. He stared at the handkerchief in amazement, muttering, "How on earth did *that* get there? S'trordinary . . ." He looked up and grinned ingratiatingly at the sentry. "I don't seem to be in funds right now. 'Course, soon as I marry the Princess Rosamund, I daresay I could offer you a tidy sum . . ." He broke off as the sentry flung open the gate quicker than you could say 'fairy story'.

"Gosh," said the prince. "Thanks awfully."

"Don't mention it," said the sentry in a tired voice, as the prince, after a small disagreement with his charger which kept going round in circles, re-mounted and rode into the courtyard.

The king was sitting on his throne in the Great Hall, eating a boiled egg. Princess Magwitch was desperately searching her account books, looking for yet more money to give away, and Princess Rosamund was

"Oh," cried Magwitch. "You poor, poor thing." And rushed to him, tearing off her patched, stained cardigan to make a pillow for his head. As she stroked his brow, trying not to spread her warts, the prince began to come round, but prudently kept his eyes shut.

"Er — are you — ehm — still there?" he said faintly.

"Ssssh," soothed Magwitch. "Of course I am . . . I won't leave you."

"I was afraid of that," said the prince, and opened his eyes just the teeniest slit. This manoeuvre didn't seem to produce any great improvement in Magwitch's looks, so he took courage by the throat and opened his eyes wide.

"Pheeew. You aren't half ugly!"

"I know," sighed Magwitch sadly, "but I'm really quite nice when you get to know me."

The king, meanwhile, was wriggling crossly on his throne. He wasn't used to being ignored.

"Oi!" he said. "You. I'm over here!"

Behind the throne, Rosamund, who was enjoying the excitement, giggled and the prince looked fearfully at Magwitch as she helped him up.

He limped fragilely over to the king and bowed, letting some more loose snow fall into his boots.

"I bring you greetings, majesty, from my father, the king, and I am here to offer," he gulped, "that is, to offer my hand in —" he looked at Magwitch out of the corner of his eye and felt sick. Still, his father has been insistent . . . "To offer my hand in marriage to the Princess Rosamund," he finished in a rush.

There was an explosion of laughter from behind the throne and Rosamund popped her head over the top, smiling angelically.

"I say, really?" she giggled. "Me? What fun." And she smiled again, the watery sunlight glancing off her gleaming white teeth.

"You?" gasped the prince, ". . . You're the Princess Rosamund?"

"Mmmm," she nodded.

"Then — who's that?" he said, turning to Magwitch.

Magwitch sniffed a drip back up her nose and smiled quietly. "I'm Magwitch, Rosamund's ugly sister." Then she smiled so sweetly that the prince surprised himself by feeling sorry for her. He patted her arm and said quietly, "Never mind, love."

Just then a maid came staggering in carrying a heavy silver tray laden with a silver tea service and porcelain cups and saucers.

""Janey!" cried Magwitch, rushing forward. "That's much too heavy for you. Let me help." But, before she reached the girl, Rosamund had stretched out a delicate foot and tripped the wretched maid, bringing her crashing to the floor in a welter of tea-leaves and broken china.

"Clumsy wench!" laughed Rosamund, in her buttery voice. "It's the dungeons for you!"

"No, please!" shrieked the little maid. Magwitch shook her fist at Rosamund. "You did that on purpose," she cried, and, turning to her father, began to plead.

"Father, you can't let her do this . . ."

"Do what?" said the king testily. "I didn't see anything. If the idiot servant broke the tea things she must be punished."

"But, Father!"

"Enough! Guards!" he shouted, clicking his fingers to summon the guards, who proceeded to drag the poor little innocent down, down, down to the dark dungeon.

Magwitch in the meantime ran by her side, clucking with concern and promising that she'd be out before you could say 'fairy story'.

Now the prince had been watching all this time, and he had begun to realise what he knew right from the start; that Rosamund was a right little devil, and Magwitch was a perfect angel. The question was, what was he going to do about it? He looked long and hard at Magwitch, who returned his look levelly from her crossed eyes, then he walked up to Magwitch and took her cold, warty hands, and kissed them.

"You're not *that* ugly," he said, softly. "In fact, you're a very beautiful person."

"So I've been told," whispered Magwitch as she blushed pinkly.

"Aha," said the king. "So that's the way of it, is it? Well, very sensible of you, if I may say so. And after all, beauty is in the eye of the beholder, isn't that what they say, eh?"

"Exactly," said the prince, dropping Magwitch's hand and turning to take Rosamund's instead. "Which is why I'll stick to this one, if you don't mind. The other one's just not beautiful enough to be my queen."

And stick to her he did.

And they lived unhappily ever after.

Which just goes to show; men are complete fools when it comes to a pretty face!

THE END

hunched on a little stool behind the throne, as close to the fire as possible, toasting her toes and wondering if her maid, whom she'd locked away in a cold dark dungeon two years ago for not ironing her shoelaces properly, would survive another winter. On the whole, she thought not, which pleased her, because then her father would let her choose another one as part of her Christmas present, and she had her eye on the cook's daughter who seemed a nice, pinchable, kickable sort of girl.

Suddenly, the great doors crashed open and, with a flourish of trumpets, the prince strode in. Magwitch, who hadn't been expecting anything of the sort, jumped and whirled round, her crossed eyes staring from her head. The prince took one look, turned chalk white, and fainted.

Continued from page 33

Neil worked in the same office as Sara . . .

IT'S NICE, SARA. I HOPE YOU AND MIKE'LL BE HAPPY.

THANKS FOR SAYING THAT, NEIL. I KNOW YOU WEREN'T VERY PLEASED AT FIRST, WHEN I STARTED GOING OUT WITH HIM.

I SUPPOSE I WAS JUST JEALOUS. I'D BEEN TRYING TO GET UP THE NERVE TO ASK YOU OUT MYSELF FOR WEEKS!

IT WAS JUST A PITY I HAD TO TAKE YOU TO THAT COFFEE BAR ON OUR FIRST DATE. MIKE WAS WORKING THERE, HE CHATTED YOU UP, AND THAT WAS THAT. EXIT, NEIL!

YOU'VE NO HARD FEELINGS, THOUGH, HAVE YOU, NEIL?

NO, OF COURSE I DON'T. THAT'S MIKE ARRIVED, ANYWAY. YOU'D BETTER GO AND GIVE HIM A KISS OR SOMETHING.

ARE YOU AS HAPPY TONIGHT AS I AM, MIKE?

HAPPIER. YOUR MUM WASN'T EXACTLY JUMPING WITH JOY WHEN SHE LET ME IN, THOUGH!

DON'T TAKE ANY NOTICE OF MUM. SHE KEEPS GOING ON ABOUT HOW I HAVEN'T KNOWN YOU LONG ENOUGH TO BE SURE WHAT YOU'RE LIKE. IF I TOOK HER ADVICE, I'D NEED TO KNOW SOMEBODY FOR 10 YEARS BEFORE I THOUGHT ABOUT GETTING ENGAGED!

SOUNDS LIKE A TYPICAL MUM. I SEE NEIL'S HERE, BY THE WAY. DID YOU HAVE TO INVITE THAT CREEP?

WHY SHOULDN'T I INVITE HIM? I ASKED EVERYBODY ELSE FROM THE OFFICE. I COULDN'T LEAVE NEIL OUT.

I JUST DON'T LIKE THE WAY HE'S ALWAYS HANGING ROUND YOU. I THINK HE STILL FANCIES YOU.

OH, MIKE, DON'T BE SILLY. HE ISN'T ALWAYS HANGING ROUND ME. WE SEE EACH OTHER IN THE OFFICE, THAT'S ALL.

Sara left Mike to mingle with the guests . . .

MIKE'S NEVER SAID ANYTHING LIKE THAT ABOUT NEIL BEFORE. IT DIDN'T OCCUR TO ME THAT HE'D MIND HIM BEING AT THE PARTY. IT JUST ISN'T LIKE MIKE TO ACT LIKE THAT . . .

Later . . .

HOW ABOUT LETTING SOMEBODY ELSE HAND OUT THE SANDWICHES FOR A WHILE, SARA? I HAVEN'T EVEN HAD A DANCE WITH YOU YET.

SURE, NEIL. I'D LOVE TO.

NO, SHE WOULDN'T. GET SOMEBODY ELSE TO DANCE WITH, MATE.

BETTER STILL, WHY DON'T YOU JUST CLEAR OFF? WE ALL KNOW YOU'VE STILL GOT YOUR EYE ON SARA. WELL, YOU HAD YOUR CHANCE WITH HER AND YOU BLEW IT! I DON'T WANT YOU HANGING ROUND HER ANY MORE.

MIKE! WHAT DO YOU THINK YOU'RE DOING?

IT'S SUPPOSED TO BE A PARTY. HE'S ENTITLED TO ASK ME TO DANCE, FOR GOODNESS' SAKE!

NOT WHEN YOU'RE ENGAGED TO ME, HE ISN'T!

IT'S OK, SARA. I THINK I'LL JUST CALL IT A NIGHT: I DON'T WANT TO CAUSE ANY TROUBLE FOR YOU.

And . . .

YOU'D NO RIGHT TO TALK TO NEIL LIKE THAT, MIKE. JUST 'COS WE'RE ENGAGED, IT DOESN'T MEAN YOU OWN ME!

I'M JUST GIVING YOU A WARNING, SARA. IF I CATCH THAT GUY WITH YOU AGAIN, I'LL GIVE HIM A THUMPING HE'LL NEVER FORGET!

But then . . .

I'M SORRY, SARA, I SHOULDN'T HAVE SHOUTED AT YOU LIKE THAT. I MUST'VE HAD TOO MUCH PUNCH OR SOMETHING. SORRY.

AND SO YOU SHOULD BE. WHAT A RIDICULOUS WAY TO BEHAVE! I HAVEN'T COMPLAINED ABOUT ALL THE GIRLS YOU'VE DANCED WITH!

The party broke up then. . .

EVERYBODY GOT EMBARRASSED WHEN MIKE STARTED SHOUTING. NO WONDER THEY COULDN'T WAIT TO LEAVE AND — OUCH! I WISH THIS RING WOULD STOP SCRATCHING MY FINGER . . .

Next day . . .

I'D BETTER GO AND SEE MIKE AT THE COFFEE BAR. I JUST HOPE HE'S IN A BETTER MOOD THAN HE WAS LAST NIGHT! IT'S FUNNY, THOUGH. USUALLY I CAN'T WAIT TO SEE HIM, BUT I DON'T FEEL LIKE THAT TODAY . . .

And . . .

I'M SORRY ABOUT LAST NIGHT, LOVE. LET'S FORGET IT HAPPENED, EH?

OK, MIKE. IF YOU SAY SO.

I STILL DON'T THINK YOU SHOULD SEE SO MUCH OF NEIL, THOUGH. I'VE SEEN THE WAY HE LOOKS AT YOU, SARA. YOU PROBABLY DON'T NOTICE IT YOURSELF, BUT I DO. HE STILL FANCIES YOU. IF YOU GAVE HIM HALF A CHANCE, HE'D BE AFTER YOU AGAIN.

I WAS NEVER REALLY HIS GIRLFRIEND, MIKE, AND I CAN'T EXACTLY AVOID HIM IN THE OFFICE. BUT, IF IT MAKES YOU FEEL ANY BETTER, I'LL TRY NOT TO GET TOO FRIENDLY WITH HIM.

Then . . .

WHAT'S UP?

IT'S THIS RING. IT SEEMS TO BE IRRITATING MY FINGER A BIT. I'M THINKING OF TAKING IT TO A JEWELLER'S TO SEE IF THEY CAN DO ANYTHING WITH IT.

HEY, I REMEMBER YOU SAYING THIS WAS YOUR AUNT'S RING, BUT I THOUGHT SHE WAS A SPINSTER?

THAT'S RIGHT. SHE WAS ENGAGED TO SOME GUY FOR ABOUT A YEAR, BUT THEY NEVER GOT MARRIED. APPARENTLY HE WAS REALLY POSSESSIVE, AND A BIT OF A FLIRT TOO. SHE TOOK IT FOR AS LONG AS SHE COULD, AND THEN SHE BROKE OFF THE ENGAGEMENT.

OH, I SEE . . .

I'M NOT SO SURE ABOUT THIS RING NOW, AND THE WAY IT KEEPS SCRATCHING MY FINGER — ALMOST LIKE A WARNING . . . AND MIKE GOT SO POSSESSIVE LAST NIGHT. HE NEVER USED TO BE LIKE THAT. I WONDER IF THE RING COULD CARRY SOME SORT OF BAD LUCK . . . ?

Continued over

A few days later . . .

SORRY, LOVE, I WON'T BE ABLE TO SEE YOU TONIGHT. THE BOSS WANTS ME TO STAY ON AND DO AN EXTRA SHIFT, OK?

I CAN'T HELP WONDERING IF THIS RING'S GOING TO BRING US BAD LUCK LIKE IT DID MIKE'S AUNT . . .

A FEW WEEKS AGO I'D HAVE BEEN REALLY DISAPPOINTED ABOUT MISSING A DATE WITH MIKE. BUT THINGS HAVE CHANGED SINCE THEN. IT MIGHT DO US BOTH GOOD TO HAVE A BREAK FROM EACH OTHER, EVEN IF IT'S ONLY FOR ONE NIGHT.

The next day . . .

YOU OUGHT TO HAVE BEEN AT THE DISCO WITH MIKE LAST NIGHT, SARA. IT WAS GREAT.

THE DISCO? MIKE COULDN'T HAVE BEEN THERE. HE WAS WORKING.

WELL, HE MUST'VE GOT AWAY EARLY OR SOMETHING. I SAW HIM THERE WITH THAT BOY TONY FROM THE COFFEE BAR.

I DON'T UNDERSTAND. MIKE DEFINITELY TOLD ME HE WAS GOING TO BE WORKING LATE! HOW COULD HE BE AT THE DISCO?

Later . . .

I'D HAVE TOLD YOU ABOUT IT MYSELF IF YOU'D GIVEN ME A CHANCE, SARA. WE FINISHED A BIT EARLIER THAN WE EXPECTED, AND TONY FANCIED A NIGHT OUT. I JUST WENT ALONG TO KEEP HIM COMPANY.

AND TO SEE WHO THE PAIR OF YOU COULD PICK UP, I SUPPOSE?

IT WAS JUST A BIT OF FUN, SARA. I DON'T KNOW WHAT'S GOT INTO YOU. YOU'RE ACTING LIKE YOU DON'T TRUST ME!

I'M NOT SURE IF I DO ANY MORE. HOW MANY OTHER NIGHTS HAVE YOU BEEN AT THE DISCO WITH TONY, WHEN I'VE THOUGHT YOU WERE WORKING?

MIKE SAID THE BOY HIS AUNT WAS ENGAGED TO WAS ALWAYS SEEING OTHER GIRLS ON THE SIDE. THIS RING'S STARTING TO SCARE ME. I CAN'T HELP FEELING IT MIGHT BRING ME THE SAME UNHAPPINESS IT BROUGHT MIKE'S AUNT.

Sara felt more and more worried about the ring — 'til one day . . .

WAIT UNTIL YOU HEAR THE JOKE NEIL TOLD ME AT LUNCHTIME, MIKE. IT'LL GIVE YOU A LAUGH.

NEIL? I THOUGHT I TOLD YOU I DIDN'T WANT YOU HAVING ANY MORE TO DO WITH THAT GUY!

YOU'RE MY GIRLFRIEND NOW. I DON'T WANT YOU HANGING AROUND WITH OTHER BLOKES, UNDERSTAND?

LET GO OF MY ARM, MIKE. YOU'RE HURTING ME! AND I DON'T LIKE IT WHEN YOU DO THIS BIG MACHO ACT!

40

I CAN'T TAKE ANY MORE OF THIS. CAN'T YOU SEE WHAT'S HAPPENING TO US? WE'RE STARTING TO ACT JUST LIKE YOUR AUNT AND THAT BOY SHE WAS ENGAGED TO!

YOU'VE BECOME JUST AS POSSESSIVE AS YOU SAID HE WAS. AND I'M ALWAYS WORRYING THAT YOU MIGHT BE SEEING OTHER GIRLS WHEN YOU'RE NOT WITH ME. IT'S BECAUSE OF THIS RING! IF WE'RE NOT CAREFUL, IT'LL DESTROY EVERYTHING WE'VE EVER FELT FOR EACH OTHER.

THERE'S SOMETHING ABOUT IT, MIKE. IT'S MADE ME FEEL UNEASY EVER SINCE I PUT IT ON. I KNOW IT SOUNDS CRAZY, BUT . . . I THINK IT'S POSSESSED IN SOME WAY.

POSSESSED? WHAT DO YOU MEAN?

POSSESSED BY THE EVIL SPIRITS OF YOUR AUNT AND THAT BOY SHE WAS ENGAGED TO.

I DON'T WANT TO WEAR IT ANY MORE, MIKE. DO YOU MIND VERY MUCH? WE CAN BUY A CHEAP RING AT THE MARKET OR SOMETHING.

OF COURSE YOU DON'T HAVE TO WEAR IT IF IT SCARES YOU, LOVE. BUT I'M NOT GETTING YOU A CHEAP RING. WE'LL WAIT TILL WE CAN AFFORD A DECENT ONE FROM THE JEWELLER'S.

I FEEL BETTER ALREADY NOW THAT I'VE TAKEN OFF THAT RING. IT'S AS IF A CURSE HAS BEEN LIFTED FROM US. THERE WAS SOMETHING EVIL ABOUT IT, I KNOW THERE WAS.

A few nights later . . .

HI, SARA. WHAT'RE YOU DOING HERE?

WAITING FOR MIKE. WE'RE GOING TO THE PICTURES.

HOW'RE YOU TWO GETTING ON THESE DAYS? I ALWAYS THOUGHT GETTING ENGAGED WAS SUPPOSED TO MAKE YOU HAPPY, BUT THAT ISN'T THE WAY YOU'VE BEEN LOOKING IN THE OFFICE.

WELL . . . WE'VE HAD ONE OR TWO PROBLEMS, I SUPPOSE. BUT I THINK EVERYTHING'S GOING TO BE OK NOW.

Then . . .

YOU CAN'T TAKE A TELLING, CAN YOU? I TOLD YOU WHAT WOULD HAPPEN IF I CAUGHT YOU WITH SARA AGAIN!

HEY! WAIT A MINUTE! I . . .

MIKE! LEAVE HIM ALONE!

Continued on page 44

41

CHRISTMAS HUN

OK, we know it's

a lot of fun most of

the time, but we thought

of a few situations

that would make you

wish that Christmas

never happened!

1. When you can't pass your little brother's room in the lead up to Christmas without him leaping out and telling you for the 47th time how much the new He-man toy is and where you can get it!

2. When your parents keep pointing out new school winter coats to you when you're out shopping with them, and you keep trying to drag them to the electrical shop to look at the new ghetto-blasters!

3. When your dad causes a power cut during Top of the Pops by trying to put the Christmas tree lights up!

4. When you've got to carry the turkey home from the butcher's — a turkey that makes you wonder if turkeys get overweight and, if so, do they get called names by their fellow gobblers?

5. When, in the middle of your latest diet, your mum starts baking yummy things like mince pies, Christmas cake and chocolate Yule logs!

6. When you can't get a wink of sleep on Christmas Eve due to your little sister leaping around her room in a state of "excitement".

7. When you wake up on Christmas morning, look at your stocking, and discover that your parents have decided to put the old saying, "when I was young all we got was an apple, an orange and a few nuts" into practice!

8. When you're dragged downstairs while half-asleep by your mum, who wants Dad to take a "loving family on Christmas morning" photograph.

9. When you find out that your parents decided to go for the winter coat (with the nice, tartan collar), instead of the ghetto-blaster (with the nice, loud, speakers).

10. When you've got to help your mum with the Christmas dinner, instead of watching "The Wizard of Oz".

11. When you "accidentally" step on your brother's new transformer space-ship and he screams for a week.

12. When your dad snores all the way through the Christmas Top of the Pops, and wakes up just in time for the boring James Bond film, which he insists on total quiet for.

13. When you've got to go to visit your "beloved relations", like your Auntie Flo, who just loves to give you some new clothes for the doll she bought you five years ago!

14. When Uncle Ralph has a bit too much Christmas cheer, and starts to do his impressions of famous Yugoslavian actors of the 70's, as well as singing "Jingle Bells" 306 times in a row!

15. When Dad starts as well!

16. When Auntie Flo decides to unveil her mince pies — a gastronomic creation that truly rivals your mum's meat-loaf in utter grossness!

17. When your mum makes you eat seven of them!

18. When you've just settled down to watch "It's a Wonderful Life" (v. weepy old Christmas film) and your dad announces that it's time for a nice family game of Trivial Pursuit!

19. When you finally get up on Boxing Day and have to face your mum and dad, who are feeling slightly "under the weather" due to the previous night's celebrations.

20. When you've got to go back to school wearing your new coat, and end up looking like a demented Eskimo, while everyone else tells you about their new stereos!

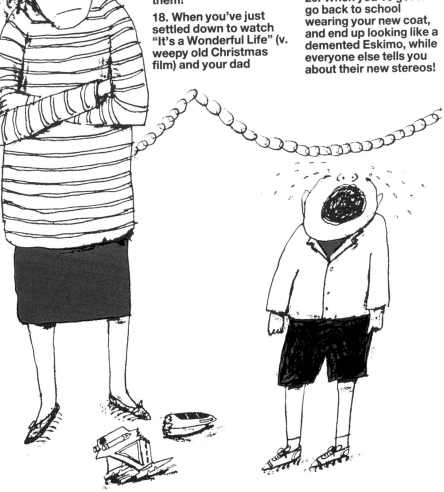

Continued from page 41

NOBODY MESSES AROUND WITH MY GIRLFRIEND! I OUGHT TO SMASH YOUR STUPID FACE IN!

STOP IT, MIKE! WHO DO YOU THINK YOU ARE? YOU CAN'T FLY INTO A TEMPER EVERY TIME I TALK TO ANOTHER BOY!

IT'S OK, SARA. DON'T WORRY ABOUT IT. I'LL SEE YOU AT THE OFFICE TOMORROW.

HOW COULD YOU ACT LIKE THAT, MIKE? YOU WERE READY TO START A FIGHT WITH NEIL, JUST BECAUSE HE WAS TALKING TO ME!

AND I'M NOT WEARING YOUR AUNT'S RING THIS TIME, AM I? I'VE BEEN AN IDIOT, MIKE. THERE WAS NOTHING OUT OF THE ORDINARY ABOUT THAT RING. THINGS WOULD HAVE BEEN JUST THE SAME, NO MATTER WHAT KIND OF RING I WAS WEARING!

WHAT DO YOU MEAN?

I'D THE SAME DOUBTS AS MY MUM AND EVERYBODY ELSE, BUT I DIDN'T WANT TO ADMIT THEM TO MYSELF. SO, INSTEAD, I BLAMED IT ALL ON THE RING.

THE RING MADE ME FEEL UNEASY FROM THE FIRST DAY I PUT IT ON. I KEPT IMAGINING IT WAS IRRITATING MY FINGER AND THAT IT CARRIED BAD LUCK, BUT IT WAS ONLY BECAUSE, DEEP DOWN, I WASN'T SURE ABOUT GETTING ENGAGED TO YOU.

IT WAS THE SAME WITH YOU, MIKE. I THOUGHT THE RING WAS CHANGING YOUR PERSONALITY — BUT IT WASN'T. I HADN'T KNOWN YOU PROPERLY WHEN WE GOT ENGAGED BUT, ONCE THE RING WAS ON MY FINGER, YOU STARTED TO LET ME SEE THE REAL YOU.

OK, SO YOU'VE SEEN THE REAL ME, BUT I STILL SAY THERE'S SOMETHING WEIRD ABOUT THAT RING.

YOU SAID YOURSELF THAT YOU FELT A LOT BETTER WHEN YOU TOOK IT OFF, DIDN'T YOU?

YES, AND I KNOW WHY, NOW. I THOUGHT IT WAS BECAUSE SOME SORT OF CURSE HAD BEEN LIFTED FROM US, BUT IT WAS NOTHING TO DO WITH THAT. IT WAS JUST THAT WITH THE RING OFF MY FINGER, I DIDN'T FEEL SO ENGAGED ANY MORE. I FELT FREE, MIKE . . . THAT'S WHAT MADE ME SO HAPPY . . .

. . . AND THAT'S WHAT I WANT NOW, MIKE . . . TO BE FREE . . .

44

I'M SORRY, MIKE. I WAS AFRAID YOUR AUNT'S RING WOULD BRING US BAD LUCK. BUT MAYBE IT BROUGHT GOOD LUCK INSTEAD . . . BECAUSE IT HELPED TO STOP US MAKING A MISTAKE WE'D ALWAYS HAVE REGRETTED . . .

THE END

POP WENT THE 80's

Well, 1990 signals the beginning of a new decade in the history of pop, but what do you remember most about the 80's? In our book, they'll be remembered for lots of things . . . animals in the charts (!), men dressing up as women, long hair and leather, Live Aid — the list is endless. Patches looks back over the past 10 years at some of the things that made us dance, swoon or guffaw heartily.

POP MUSIC in the early 80's consisted of varying factions . . . New Romantic, Futurist and a Ska revival. Ska originated in the West Indies about 30 years ago, but it was those British nutty boys, Madness, who led a pack that included The Specials, The Beat and Selector. This also seemed to overlap with a Mod revival which brought about a new interest in white R'n'B bands like Secret Affair, The Lambrettas and The Jam.

By the mid-80's, it had all but died away. However, The Specials were to feature in the charts again, as The Special AKA, when Jerry Dammers penned the classic anti-apartheid anthem, "Free Nelson Mandela".

Madness, who had released their first single, "The Prince", in 1979, eventually split in 1987 but reformed, in a more condensed version, as The Madness in 1988. Ex-drummer Woody (Daniel Woodgate) had joined Voice Of The Beehive.

Perhaps the most memorable band from the New Romantic era was Duran Duran. They caused a sensation when they entered the chart at No. 1 with "Is There Something I Should Know" in 1983. They later split into two separate

45

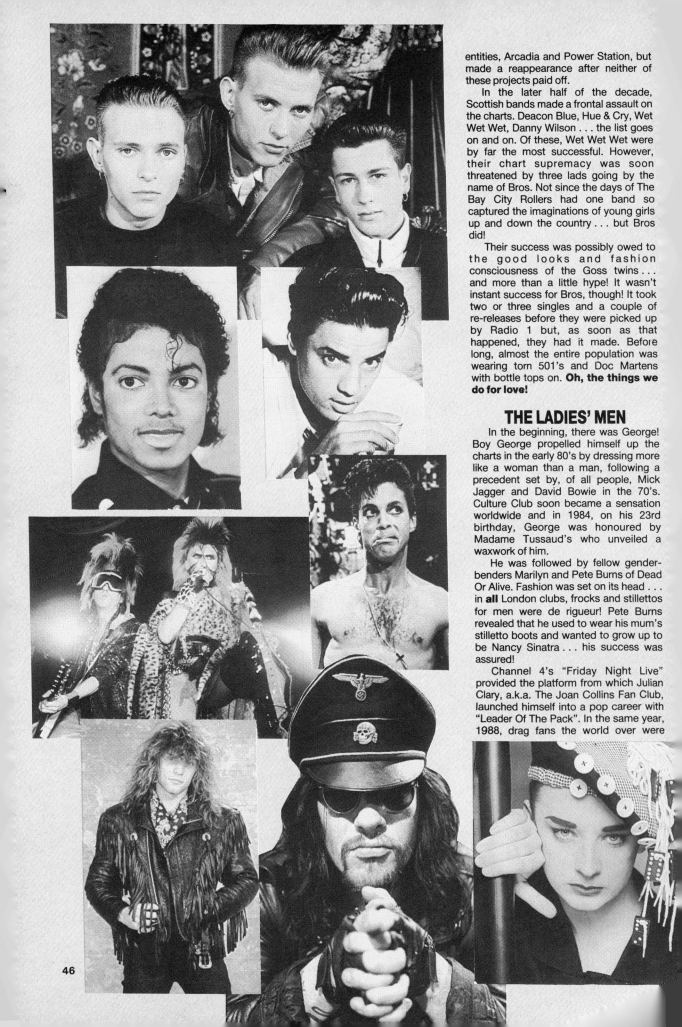

entities, Arcadia and Power Station, but made a reappearance after neither of these projects paid off.

In the later half of the decade, Scottish bands made a frontal assault on the charts. Deacon Blue, Hue & Cry, Wet Wet Wet, Danny Wilson . . . the list goes on and on. Of these, Wet Wet Wet were by far the most successful. However, their chart supremacy was soon threatened by three lads going by the name of Bros. Not since the days of The Bay City Rollers had one band so captured the imaginations of young girls up and down the country . . . but Bros did!

Their success was possibly owed to the good looks and fashion consciousness of the Goss twins . . . and more than a little hype! It wasn't instant success for Bros, though! It took two or three singles and a couple of re-releases before they were picked up by Radio 1 but, as soon as that happened, they had it made. Before long, almost the entire population was wearing torn 501's and Doc Martens with bottle tops on. **Oh, the things we do for love!**

THE LADIES' MEN

In the beginning, there was George! Boy George propelled himself up the charts in the early 80's by dressing more like a woman than a man, following a precedent set by, of all people, Mick Jagger and David Bowie in the 70's. Culture Club soon became a sensation worldwide and in 1984, on his 23rd birthday, George was honoured by Madame Tussaud's who unveiled a waxwork of him.

He was followed by fellow gender-benders Marilyn and Pete Burns of Dead Or Alive. Fashion was set on its head . . . in **all** London clubs, frocks and stillettos for men were de rigueur! Pete Burns revealed that he used to wear his mum's stilletto boots and wanted to grow up to be Nancy Sinatra . . . his success was assured!

Channel 4's "Friday Night Live" provided the platform from which Julian Clary, a.k.a. The Joan Collins Fan Club, launched himself into a pop career with "Leader Of The Pack". In the same year, 1988, drag fans the world over were shocked to hear of the death of the **ultimate** gender-bender, Divine.

THE YOBS, SLOBS AND GLAMOUR JOBS

The 80's just caught the tail end of the punk era and seemed set to become the era of heavy metal. The New Wave Of British Heavy Metal produced such bands as Iron Maiden, Saxon, Judas Priest and Def Leppard who set the pace for Motorhead and the Deep Purple splinter groups, Gillan, Whitesnake and Rainbow.

By 1984, however, most of the early drive was lost and HM rarely featured in the charts. It was about this time that Sigue Sigue Sputnik were sprung on an unsuspecting public. With almost as much publicity in the space of three months as the Royal Family have in a year, the Sputniks rocketted to the No. 1 spot. Rock 'n' Roll was back in a big way!

Bon Jovi, who had spent years building a massive following in the States, smashed their way into the UK charts in 1986. They headed a new rock revival whose prime movers included Europe and Def Leppard . . . pop music for metal muthas!

In the late 80's, there was another rock undercurrent, going by the name Grebo Rock. The **Prime Mover** in this case was Zodiac Mindwarp. Other rock genres included Speed Metal and Thrash Metal . . . with such unlikely sounding proponents as Suicidal Tendencies, Napalm Death, Megadeth, and Cryptic Slaughter (!).

COMMERCIAL SUCCESSES

One novelty which was introduced during the late 80's was the bright idea of using "golden oldies" to sell jeans on TV. Levi 501's were reintroduced to a fashion-conscious public with accompaniment of classic tracks from Marvin Gaye, "Heard It Through The Grapevine", and Sam Cooke, "Wonderful World". Both tracks, released as singles, shot up the charts and the trouser-dropping model from the ad with the Marvin Gaye soundtrack became an instant heart-throb. His name . . . Nick Kamen! Soon, he was signed to WEA for his first single, "Each Time You Break My Heart", which got *too* far up the charts!

The next series of ads featured Sharon Sheeley's true-life romance story about Eddie Cochran. Needless to say, Eddie Cochran soon charted posthumously. Sam Cooke did the same when "When A Man Loves A Woman" was released. Even Muddy Waters, the venerated master of Chicago blues, saw chart success when the 1977 recording of his classic "Mannish Boy" was the backing to a Levi plug. All in all, it was possibly the most successful advertising campaign of the 80's and had record companies everywhere scouring their back catalogues for money-spinners.

GOING SOLO

The 1980's raised a few solo artists to legendary status, not least Michael Jackson. Michael has sold more albums than any other artist to date and, in 1988, embarked on one of the most comprehensive world tours in history. Between them, the albums "Thriller" and "Bad" sold over 50 million copies and made life quite cushy for our Mike.

George Michael first appeared on the scene in the 80's, along with his partner, Andrew Ridgeley, in Wham! When they split after a farewell gig at Wembley Arena, George went on to a successful solo career while Andy slipped into obscurity. George's first solo album, "Faith", sold millions and guaranteed his future.

Madonna Ciccone came from nowhere to leave a trail of platinum albums all over the globe. Films followed . . . namely, "Desperately Seeking Susan", "Shanghai Surprise" and "Who's That Girl?". After a world tour, Madonna took a break from singing to concentrate on acting before stepping back into the studio to resume her pop career.

Prince also made the link between music and film with "Purple Rain" and "Sign O' The Times". Hailed by some as the greatest genius pop has ever seen and branded a pornographer by others,

one thing is certain . . . Prince was one of the biggest influences on the music of the late 80's.

A DAY TO REMEMBER . . . AND FACES TO FORGET

Possibly the most memorable day of the entire decade was the day in 1985 when billions of people all over the world tuned in to watch Live Aid from Wembley Stadium, London and JFK Stadium, Philadelphia. Bob Geldof was hailed as a saint for organising an event which raised £53 million for famine relief in the Sudan. There can't have been a dry eye anywhere in the world when David Bowie introduced a short film, set to the music of The Cars, which left no doubt in people's minds about the catastrophe in Africa.

One name which will probably not spring to mind immediately is that of Owen Paul. Just for the record, he was a Glasgow Celtic football player who decided to have a go at being a pop star. Two singles later he was back to playing football . . . need we say more?

Paul King bounded into the charts on a pair of gaudy Dr Martens and hung around for a while before bouncing straight out again. Bit unfortunate, really, 'cos their first couple of singles were quite good. Still, that's pop for you!

Now, about this animal that charted! Anyone remember that cuddly chap Roland Rat? He was great when he appeared on Breakfast TV but unfortunately his "people" decided he should make a record . . . not a very clever idea! UB40 later honoured him with the ballad, "Rat In Mi Kitchen". Ahem! ◆

THERE'S A FIRST FOR EVERYTHING

IT'S FINALLY HAPPENED! THE HUNKY CAPTAIN OF THE FOOTBALL TEAM (THE ONE YOU'VE BEEN DROPPING BOOKS IN FRONT OF FOR MONTHS) HAS ASKED YOU OUT. YIPPEE! HURRAH! OH NO, WHAT DO YOU DO NOW?

After the initial wave of ecstacy, a feeling of despair and dread usually sets in.

What'll you wear?

What'll you say to him?

What happens if he doesn't turn up?

What if he turns up and the whole evening's a disaster?

Well . . . don't panic! This may be little comfort for you just now, but remember, this is going to be one of the most memorable nights of your life, so make the most of it. When it's all over, you'll wonder what you were so worried about.

BE PREPARED

Start by making sure that whatever you're wearing is clean and ironed. Have a nice relaxing bath and wash your hair, conditioning it afterwards.

Dry and style your hair in a way that suits you and doesn't need constant teasing/flattening/fluffing up or lots of hairspray. There's nothing that's going to put a boy off more than a mouthful of rock hard lacquered hair when he tries to kiss you and misses!

Cleanse, tone and moisturise your face and neck. Then apply your favourite shades of make-up. Don't be too heavy-handed and make sure everything is blended in perfectly. This isn't the time to experiment with new colours or techniques; what would happen if it went all wrong? Stick to what suits you, and to easy, basic beauty techniques.

SHOULD YOU TELL YOUR PARENTS?

This can be a tricky decision if your parents have stated that they're against you having boyfriends. But you should consider the point that honesty is the best policy. Your parents would be hurt and lose their trust in you if they found you dating behind their backs. Not to mention the fact that they'd probably never let you out of the house again until you were 95!

However, if you have decided to tell them and if you're worried about their reaction, tell them as tactfully but as honestly as you can. Just say that so and so has asked you out and you'd like to go. Be mature and responsible about the situation, especially if they are against it. This may sound hard to do, but they may be pleasantly surprised to see you appreciating their opinions. If they say no — screaming, weeping and sulking will just prove their point that you're too young for something like this. Why not try and compromise? Corny though it may seem, why not suggest that he comes to pick you up from your house so your parents can meet him?

WHAT TO WEAR

Of course, this all depends on where you're going, but there's really only one rule about what to wear — something in which you're comfortable and which you know makes you look good. Here are some points to consider:

* Avoid mini-skirts which wander up when you're sitting down and tops which slip off the shoulders, or reveal a bit too much bust. This would give your date the wrong impression — especially on the first night!

* If you tend to get all hot and clammy when you're nervous, avoid wearing layers of clothes. Choose something made from cotton, as this is absorbent.

* If you're planning to take a moonlit stroll in the park, don't wear high heels. There's nothing more unromantic than

TIME
. .!

staggering or clumping along gravel paths, dragging stiletto heels out of the mud or cracks between the pavement.

WHAT HAPPENS IF HE DOESN'T TURN UP?

It's best not to think about this but, unfortunately, this situation does happen to some of us. If it does happen to you there are a few things you could do:
* You could phone him to see where he is (this is only for the very brave). If you do get him on the phone and he admits that he's changed his mind about you, try your hardest to be calm. Say to him that it would have been decent of him if he could have phoned to tell you and then that you'll see him around.
* You could dash off and see your best friend. She'll be a shoulder to cry on, and will make you feel loads better and more able to face him when you see him.
* You could go home. This'll mean that your parents will realise what has happened (if you've told them) and it may be a bit embarrassing appearing 'jilted'. But at least your family will rally round you and you'll feel better!

WHAT SHOULD I SAY?

This is a very common worry, but it is easily solved. When he comes round for you, or you meet him somewhere, you don't have to say that much — a smile usually says it all. Just remember, though, that he'll be quite nervous too. Why not try mapping out a few possible topics of conversation the night before? Music, films, how much homework you've got — the list is endless.

It can be a help if you're going somewhere definite, like the pictures or a disco, then you can start the conversation about that. If you're stuck, why not ask questions about him (boys love talking about themselves!)? If you try to relax, you'll find the words will flow so much easier.

AT THE END OF THE NIGHT

So, it's the end of a perfect/dreadful evening. What should you do?

Well, if everything that's happened has been a total disaster, and you're desperate to go home, try to be as polite about it as possible. You may be tempted to run away from him, but just think how you'd feel if he dashed off? If you really don't fancy a kiss goodnight, just say that you have to go now, say thanks, then give him a peck on the cheek.

However, if you've enjoyed yourself and it's obvious that he has too, just relax and let what happens happen! This may be the first time you've kissed but, as you'll soon find out, to enjoy this pleasant sensation it's essential that you relax and take your time.

The first kiss is normally something which you've fantasised about, and often it's a bit of a disappointment when it actually happens. But kissing improves with practise, so if it's a bit fumbly and embarrassing, don't worry. Time and experience will improve matters no end!

Don't worry about the first kiss — just relax, act naturally and get on with enjoying it!

Your date may suggest seeing you again but, if he doesn't, don't think that emigrating would be the easy answer. Some guys prefer to wait till the next time they see the girl in question before asking her out again (but don't ask *us* why!).

And, anyway, if nothing ever does come of it, don't let it get to you. Remember the old saying — "there're plenty more fish in the sea"!

CHEAP TRICKS!!

HOW CAN YOU LOOK LUSCIOUS AND LOVELY WHEN YOU'VE ONLY 17p IN YOUR PURSE? WELL, IT'S MUCH EASIER THAN YOU'D THINK. IF YOU WANT TO MAKE WHAT YOU HAVE GOT SPIN OUT, OR TAKE ADVANTAGE OF WHAT'S IN THE KITCHEN, WELL — HERE'S HOW . . .

MAKE-UP

Always apply your foundation with a damp sponge. Not only will it be easier to blend but you'll use a lot less foundation.

If you find that you're having difficulty squeezing the last of your foundation out of the tube, cut the end off with a pair of scissors.

If you've made the mistake of buying a foundation which is too dark, add a little to some face cream, and use it as a tinted moisturiser.

Brushing on face powder does leave a smoother cover but there's a lot of waste. If you're running low, put it on using a ball of cotton wool.

If you're totally out of face powder, use a light dusting of baby powder. Don't be too heavy-handed, though, and avoid this if your skin is very dry or easily irritated.

Your eyeshadow will also last longer if you apply it with a brush. More ends up on the eyelid if you do use a brush rather than a sponge applicator.

If you run out of eyeshadow, dust your eyelids lightly with face powder and a slight touch of your blusher.

If your eyeliner's become so short you can't even hold it, outline your eyes with some mascara, using a fine brush.

Keep your eyeliner pencils in the fridge. They'll be easier to sharpen if they're cool.

If you run out of blusher, make some cream blusher. Just mix some lipstick and a little cold cream in the palm of your hand and apply over your foundation.

Vaseline makes an excellent lip gloss or balm.

Applying your lipstick with a lip brush not only leaves a better finish, but you use a lot less than if you use it in stick form.

TEETH

Use salt (yeuch!) or bicarbonate of soda if you run out of toothpaste. Surprisingly they both give excellent results.

Whiten your teeth by moistening your brush with lemon juice, then dipping it into bicarbonate of soda.

SKIN

Rinse an oily skin with lemon or orange juice, then pat it off with dampened cotton wool.

Save on cleanser by using half the amount you'd normally use but apply it with dampened cotton wool to make it go further.

Use yoghurt as a face mask. It'll leave your skin feeling soft and fresh looking.

If you're out of cleanser, dip a cotton wool pad into milk. It'll remove oil and grime and leave your skin feeling soft and smooth.

Oatmeal and milk mixed together, applied and left on your face, will deep cleanse your face. Whilst removing, rub gently and you'll exfoliate your skin too.

Steep orange peel in boiling water, leave to cool and then use as a toner. Store in the fridge.

HAIR

Oatmeal and talcum powder can be used as a dry shampoo. Leave it in your hair for 10 minutes, then brush out thoroughly.

If you're out of conditioner, try natural yoghurt which'll add body and shine. Or why not rinse your hair with wine and lemon juice if it's prone to greasiness?

If you'd like to try a deep conditioner for very dry hair but can't afford to fork out for one, borrow some of your mum's olive oil and massage it into your hair and scalp. Wrap a damp towel around your head and leave for twenty minutes, then shampoo twice.

Warm and mix a few of your odds and ends of lipstick and put into tiny pots. Apply with a lip brush.

BROTHERS

I was getting sick of being Steve's brother; he was the brainy, good-looking athletic type that all the girls fancied. Me? Well, I was a weed . . . then I decided to do something about it . . .

"STEVE'S the best forward we've had in years!"

"You don't have to tell me. I know!"

Chris laughed. He didn't really get it — me being Steve's kid brother and what I have to live with. How can he? He only has a sister and she has a Sindy doll, not a fan-club. On the other hand, the brainy, macho-looking star of the soccer team has all the girls in school ready to kiss the hem of his shorts.

"Sorry, mate. Must be depressing following an act like that."

"Yeah. I could stick the sporting image if he wasn't such a box-office draw with types like her . . ." I nodded to where Andrea Mollins was standing, all blonde hair and terrific legs and nervously chewing her scarf to bits as she watched.

Chris shook his head. "Imagine what it must be like having a girl like that willing to freeze to death on the touchline just to cheer on your performance."

As we imagined, the final whistle blew and Andrea ran onto the pitch to chuck herself onto Steve's sweaty shirt, all adoration. It was enough to make you vomit, so we headed off towards the main gates, heads down in the wind.

"What's wrong with me, Chris? Girls never notice me — it's always him. It's like I'm nearly invisible."

"It's because you're so skinny," Chris grinned. "Come on, I'll race you to the café. Loser buys the bacon sarnies . . ."

I legged it after him even though I'd no chance — he zooms along like Seb Coe. "Skinny is bad news," I thought as I leaped over the litter on the pavement, "but I reckon I'm boring. I have the same effect on people as the shipping forecast . . . their eyes start to glaze over."

Of course, Chris said it was a load of cobblers, but he was my mate. To most of the kids in school I was Steve Brinton's brother. Not Tom Brinton. Not Tom. Just 'Steve's brother'. The ultimate non-person.

"Quit scowling and get your

IN ARMS!

mouth round these," Chris said, banging down a plateful of sarnies. The smell was great.

"Don't look now," Chris said, "but Gill Smethers is over in the corner and she's looking at you like you're the bargain of the week."

I didn't look. I just muttered, "So what?" I'd nothing special against the girl except she'd been out with every lad in the fifth year, so if she was down to me she was a bit desperate.

"You could be a shade more enthusiastic. She's not exactly Andrea standard, but you've got to start somewhere. You've been moaning on for months about girls looking right through you. Well, she's not. I think she fancies you. Besides — she's available. If you keep lusting after the ones with boyfriends, you'll never make it."

He was right, I supposed. I glanced over to where she was sitting and she flashed me an enormous grin which even I could recognise as a green-light signal.

"Go, boy," I thought. "She's not Andrea, but you need to get your balance ... go chat her up."

I didn't, though. I was scared her spotty mate would earwig and start sending me up, so I left it till later and phoned her.

"Brilliant," she breathed huskily, like my suggestion of going to the pictures was the most original idea since the invention of the wheel.

Of course, I should've realised it wasn't me she was interested in — she hardly looked at me all night, except to ask for more to eat and what wonderboy Steve was up to.

Once she'd gnashed her way through three King Cones, two hot dogs and a packet of marshmallows I thought she'd be full, but no luck — she started dropping hints about stopping at the chippy on the way home.

"We'll miss your bus," I said, steering her firmly down the road.

"Oh, I told my dad to pick me up at your house later," she said.

I thought it was a bit odd but I didn't catch on. Not then. Not till we got to the house. Then she started.

"Where's Steve?"

I shrugged. "I suppose he's in the kitchen with Andrea," then added "... his girlfriend."

That didn't stop her, though. She raced in and before I even reached the kitchen I could hear her warbling on to Steve.

Her voice went on and on and it finally dawned on me. She'd just got

me to take her out so she could get back here and chat him up. As if he'd want anything to do with a loud-mouthed cow like her! I should have known!

Steve thought so too. He was flashing death-ray messages in my direction but I was too depressed to care. I sat hunched in the corner of the settee and switched my mind over to fantasy ...

I pretended Andrea was secretly madly in love with me and pretty soon she'd be forced to confess her feelings ... I was in heaven until Gill's dad pounded on the door to collect her and let us all off the hook.

I gave girls a miss for quite a while after that.

"I'm going to get stuck into some serious weight-training," I told Chris. "Then maybe I'll get girls who fancy me, not him!"

"You can anyway," he said. "You undersell yourself, that's all."

I realised he was right, but I sold my BMX and bought a set of weights anyway.

It nearly drove Dad stark raving bonkers. He was always fairly unpleasant about my drum practice because my thumping away gave him a massive headache, but the hundred press-ups per night plus this ace skipping routine I worked out caused more than one mega-snap over the next month or two.

He ranted on about studying for exams and planning a good, worthwhile career, but I just shut my ears because I already knew how the exams would go. Badly. Even if I scraped through, my marks would look pathetic next to Steve's. They always did. I hadn't bothered trying this year because I'd reckoned it wasn't worth it. I'd be bound to fail.

All the same it was a shock when I found out I'd failed the lot. Even Dozy Deakin had better grades than me!

Steve, of course, was furious. "I don't rate having a dumbo for a brother, Tom!"

"Tough!" I said. I'd been messing about a lot in class. When you don't listen or take notes you can dream up some interesting diversions ... things that make everybody laugh or just notice you even.

Steve could lean on me all he liked, I didn't care.

"What about your dad, though? He'll nail you to the carpet," Chris said later. We were in the library.

He was copying out some essay or other and I was peeling an orange and working out how to get enough cash to go to the Starlight disco on Saturday.

"Don't worry about me. I'm used to being bawled at."

"...and then he superglued Mr Haver's jacket to the desk! It was so funny, Julie, you'd have died!"

I recognised the voice from the other side of the shelves as a girl in our class — Beverley Harper, pretty girl but dead quiet and I'd thought she was totally appalled by my little joke in Tuesday's French lesson.

"He's not bad-looking either." It was Beverley again. I strained my ears to catch what they were saying.

"Mmmm," murmured Julie who-ever-she-was, "and didn't you say he was Steve Brinton's brother? Now, he's something else!"

What was the use?

* * * *

"What do you mean play in a band? What band? When? Are you completely crazy, lad?"

I knew he'd flip his lid, especially since the gory scenes over my mock results, but I was determined to win this one.

"It's just a local group, Dad. They need a drummer and it's only weekends. It's not like I'm going on the road!"

"You'll end up digging the road if you don't get some homework done!"

"I'll fit it in, Dad. Like Steve does. He's out all the time with Andrea and no-one gives him a hard time for it."

"Because he gets good marks, Tom," Mum put in.

"What about all the time he takes playing football, then?"

"We can't stop something he has a genuine talent for."

"And how d'you know I haven't got a genuine talent for drumming?" I shouted. He must've felt guilty because he shut up.

It was the best thing that had happened since I measured myself against the bedroom door (another 3 cm.!). We'd been hanging about at the Starlight when this guy came over. Denny, they called him, and he was lead guitar with the group that played there.

"Aren't you the guy who sat in with us for a while last week?" he said.

I nodded. "I did a couple of numbers. It was great. I'd never played with a proper group before... I just mess about..."

"How d'you fancy playing regularly then — until our drummer's out of hospital?" he drawled.

I was speechless. I couldn't believe my luck. Nothing would stop me grabbing this chance with both hands, not even Dad.

He never actually agreed, but he didn't say no either so I was there, at the Starlight, every Friday and Saturday having the best time ever.

"You should hear what some of the girls in school have been saying about you," Chris said. "I spent half an hour chatting up that redhead in fourth year and she kept dragging the subject round to you."

"You're joking!"

He shrugged. "She seemed impressed..."

I wasn't. I'd heard girls talk before and it wasn't me they were impressed with — just the things I did. Besides, I couldn't concentrate on Chris's gossip; I had other things to think about, problems of my own... and one problem in particular.

It all blew up because I went to this party at Denny's.

I shouldn't have gone really. The Starlight closed at one o'clock and, if I'd any sense I'd have gone home, but Denny kept on at me — making out I'd be chicken if I didn't. So I did.

I eventually ended up arm wrestling this gorilla (God knows why) with a mob round us yelling encouragement.

Now was the time to see if the weight training had paid off, and it had. I got kind of punch-drunk with my little success. Suddenly I was the centre of attention. A couple of girls appeared as if by magic and started feeling my arm muscles while someone else thrust two wooden spoons in my hand, saying, "Give us a solo, Tom!"

I did and they loved it.

"You really are brilliant at that, you know," said a familiar voice. I swung round.

"Andrea! I didn't know you were here. Where's Steve?"

She smiled her photographic-model smile and put her hands on my shoulders.

"I don't know. Probably fast asleep by now. I thought I'd prefer to come to this party alone... Chris told me you'd be here."

"What? Look, maybe I'm getting the wrong idea," I stammered.

"I doubt it," Andrea said. "I very much doubt it," she breathed, moving closer and smelling wonderful.

"What about Steve?"

She lowered her long eyelashes and shrugged. "Oh, I don't know. People change, don't they? Some relationships just grind to a halt."

I thought, "This isn't happening — you've tuned into the fantasy-channel by mistake..."

She had both arms around me by this time. All the bright light and noise seemed to have melted into blackness and I was dancing with Andrea to this smoochy music...

"So there I am with Andrea," I told Chris. Well, I had to tell somebody, I'd have burst otherwise!

"Go on then — get to the double X-rated bits."

"That's just it. Instead of grabbing my chances, what do I do? I back off — I practically said 'no thanks' like she was a second helping of chocolate gateau or something."

"Why?" Chris asked, puzzled.

"I don't know, honestly. I just know she chucked herself at me and I kept thinking she's Steve's girl. She's making a real plonker of him behind his back, and it turned me right off."

"You'd have been one up on Steve, though. Wouldn't it have been worth it?"

"No, if she makes him look an idiot — she's sort of making me look one too... him being my brother."

Chris shook his head. "That's a new one. You blew up when he told you your exam results reflected on him, but now you're identifying with the smoothie. Very confusing..."

I was about to confess that I actually felt sorry for Steve when this girl walks in. Fantastic looking she was — gazing about in that helpless way new girls do, and pushing her hands through a mass of blonde hair.

"Eat your heart out, Kim Wilde," Chris muttered as about 15 guys fell over each other in the rush to show her which locker to use and all that. We both lost interest in Steve's love life and spent the next day or two super-glued to the honey-pot's tail like a couple of MI5 agents. We didn't get far, other than her name was Kathy.

"She's aleady asked around about Steve," Chris groaned. "Talk about jammy! He timed finishing with Andrea dead right."

Possibly, but it seemed to make him about as happy as an abcessed tooth when she called it off.

"Aw, leave it out, Steve," I said. "She's not worth you getting depressed."

"How do you know what she's worth? She was my girlfriend, not yours."

I bit my lip. I could've told him what a two-faced cow she turned out to be, but I didn't. I just said, "She's not worth you crashing your 'A' levels, is she? If you don't get on with your swotting you might not get good enough grades for medical school . . ."

"Swotting?" he shouted. "That's

good coming from you. When did you last do a stroke of work? The rate you're going at you'll be expelled!"

"I'm leaving at the end of term," I said flatly.

Steve blew up. "What? I bet you haven't told Dad — he'll be mad when he finds out you're going on the dole."

"Who said anything about going on the dole?" I snapped. "I'll get a job."

"What as? All you can do is bang your ruler on the off beat."

I hit him.

It was only a little scrap. Nothing serious. Just a mutual airing of feelings in a brotherly way and Dad pulled us apart as usual — but there was one difference: I was winning.

* * * *

"So now you can beat him," Chris said thoughtfully, "and you're not worried about qualifications!"

"No," I grinned. "They don't ask your maths grade in a recording studio."

"If you're so confident, why don't you get stuck into chatting up Kathy Saunders while your Steve's still sticking plasters on his black eye and broken heart!"

"With my track record?" I muttered. "I've not had all that much practice, remember."

"Don't look now," Chris whispered, "but here comes Kathy now."

I turned on my heel to face her.

"Hi, Kathy! Where are you off to?"

"Oh, I'm just going up to watch the football team practise. I heard you've got a brilliant team here."

"The best," Chris said dully as we turned the corner into the main

corridor and Kathy trotted off to watch Steve and his mates.

"She's keen on soccer . . . perhaps that's all they have in common . . ." I mumbled.

"If you believe that, you'll believe anything."

It was hard to know what to believe as the days went by. Kathy had half the upper school guessing. No-one knew who she really fancied, not even Moira Hill, the 'lovematch mastermind'.

"All I can tell you is Kathy's not really into serious relationships," she said.

She came to the Starlight at weekends and danced with lots of different guys, but no-one knew who she really liked.

"I reckon Kathy Saunders is playing games," I overheard one of the girls say as I was passing the bar. "She's got her eye on somebody . . . but I can't decide who . . . maybe one of the Brinton brothers — but I don't know which one . . ."

The Brinton brothers. I liked it.

I found Steve at the end of the bar.

"Kathy's been gone a good ten or fifteen minutes. I thought she was with you."

I took a swallow. "No such luck," I moaned.

"She seems to fancy you, though . . . or so some of the lads say."

I looked down at my glass. "Some say it's you she's after."

We grinned at each other.

"We'll have to sort something out. Fancying the same girl is bad news," Steve said. "It's bad for my image when gorgeous girls prefer you to me!"

I laughed, but then I saw the astonished look on Steve's face. I turned to see what he was looking at and my chin bounced off the floor.

It was Chris. He had his arm around Kathy Stockton and she was gazing at him like she'd just won him in a prize raffle.

"The rat! He never breathed a word and he's my best mate."

"Maybe he only just found out — she was a bit secretive."

I shrugged, then I started to laugh. "Just think, Steve, us both fancying her and she goes off with Chris. Typical!"

Steve laughed too. "Yeah, while we were working on our images, Chris was working on Kathy. The jammy devil's plan paid off, too!"

I sighed and leaned back on the bar just as a couple of girls passed . . . pretty girls. One of them looked over her shoulder and smiled. At me? Or at Steve?

"The night's not over yet, is it, Tom?" Steve winked.

I shook my head happily. After all, Kathy, Andrea and Gill weren't the only girls in the world and we could still have a great time . . . me and my brother.

THE END.

IT WASN"

EVERYONE, AT SOME POINT OR OTHER, HAS AN EXPERIENCE WHICH COULD BE CONSIDERED TO BE AN "AWKWARD SITUATION". THE TRICK IS LEARNING HOW TO DEAL WITH THEM ON THE SPOT *AND* COME OUT ON TOP. SOMETIMES THE SOLUTION TO AN EMBARRASSING PROBLEM CAN BE AS OBVIOUS AS THE NOSE ON YOUR FACE BUT, IN SOME INSTANCES, IT CAN BE AS DIFFICULT TO WORM YOUR WAY OUT OF A SITUATION AS IT WAS EASY TO FALL INTO IT . . .

SUPPOSE you accidentally wander into the men's room instead of the ladies' on your first day at college? Thankfully, it's deserted, but, on your panicked exit, you bump into a young gent who appears even more startled by your presence than you are by his. What do you do? Scream? Dash out with your hands over your face? Or, quietly assure him that this is actually the ladies' and some practical joker must've switched the door signs?

This process of transferring the embarrassment from yourself to some hapless stooge obviously involves a lot of quick thinking and a little lie telling. Another method involves the unwitting co-operation of a friend. Picture the scene . . .

You're walking through town with a friend. You stop to look at a display of shoes outside a shop. As you start to walk away, your bag gets caught in the display rack and the whole lot comes crashing down about you! Your friend freezes, turns to look at you with an expression of sheer horror on her face . . . time for you to act! Before anyone notices what is happening, silently mouth the word "RUN" to your friend and, as she takes to her heels, do a quick about-turn and stroll leisurely in the opposite direction. The irate shop assistant will, nine times out of ten, chase the first person he sees running away!

There is, of course, the honest approach. George Washington pioneered this one! According to popular legend, young George was sitting around bored while his father was out doing the things that fathers do. Suddenly, an idea sprang into his mind! He'd do his dad an enormous favour by chopping down the cherry tree in the back yard. However, when Mr Washington returned from his day's business, he was far from delighted to see his prized tree reduced to a log and set about tracking down the culprit. When confronted, young George replied that he couldn't tell a lie and yes, he was responsible. The story goes on to say that his father, pleased that George had been honest with him, refrained from giving his son the kind of trouncing he might have

expected. Needless to say, this one tends not to be too well received these days and our considered opinion is, IF IN DOUBT, "FABRICATE"!

It's summertime and your parents have gone off for a week and left you in charge of the house. Your best mate comes to stay with you, the first day has been riotous and hilarious . . . and not one single inch of the house has been burnt to a cinder or stolen because you left the front door open while you were out sunbathing! Unfortunately, precisely 24 hours after your parents left, your dad's beloved canary decides, quite inconsiderately, that it's time for it to curl up its tootsies and keep its appointment with its Maker. Although its food dish was full and it had plenty water, you know exactly who'll be held responsible . . . that's right, YOU! The solution here is pretty straightforward . . . provided that you're prepared to abandon all scruples!

First of all, remove the bird's perch from the cage, gently wrap the deceased's claws around the perch (you can use wire for this bit if you need to) and carefully place it in the freezer.

Now, on the day your parents are due home, begin part two of the plan. Ensure that the food dish and water bottle in the cage are replenished, remove the canary and perch from the freezer. (If you used wire, remove it and you should find that Tweetie Pie sits there quite happily!) Stick the perch back in the cage and, when you see the car drawing up, start whistling like a canary and rattle the bars of

the cage slightly. This'll make your folks think that the bird's glad to see them home but, just as they enter the sitting room, the ice will have melted and Tweetie Pie will be seen falling off his perch onto the bottom of the cage. Obviously the poor thing couldn't stand the excitement, eh? The alternative is to buy an identical canary!

To see how you measure up, try out this simple test and see how well you score . . .

1. On your way home one evening, you get caught in a thunderstorm, so you start pounding down the road towards home before you're completely drenched. Unfortunately, it's raining so hard that you can't see properly and rush through the front door of the house three doors up from you where they seem to be holding a birthday celebration. Needless to say, they're slightly taken aback at your entrance . . . what do you do?
a) Beg forgiveness and leave sheepishly,
b) Tell them you're sorry for interrupting, but you're locked out and could you borrow a towel, or,
c) Announce that you're a surprise "Dripogram" and launch into a spluttery rendition of "Happy Birthday"?!

2. There's this guy at school you really fancy but you never get a chance to speak to him. However, you've just spotted him, on his own, in the corridor. You rush over to say a few well-chosen words but, on your way, somehow manage to wrap the strap of your bag around your legs and

ME!

end up on the floor at his feet. Your next move?
a) Crawl frantically 'round the corner and into the first hole you find,
b) Grab him by the ankles and start kissing his shoes, all the while telling him how much you've admired him from afar, or
c) Howl a piece of prime mourning from the school's Easter Passion Play while mopping at his feet with your hair and holding out a card declaring that you're free for pantomimes?

3. Mum and Dad are going out for the evening and you assure them that you'll be all right staying in, all on your own, to do some homework. Little do they know that as soon as they're out of the door your boyfriend gives the secret knock at the back door and is in the house within seconds. Unfortunately, things don't go as planned for Mum and Dad's evening out and they return home early to find you and the aforementioned boyfriend indulging in some serious snogging on the couch. An explanation is expected . . .
a) "Erm, sorry, Mum . . . I don't know what came over us! I won't (sob!) let it (boo hoo!) happen (weep!) again . . . HONEST!",
b) "Actually, we were rehearsing the seduction scene from 'The Taming Of The Shrew' . . .", or,
c) "Well, we were discussing lycanthropy, — THAT'S WEREWOLVES TO YOU — for a history project on 'Peasant Superstitions of Eastern Europe In The 15th Century', and were merely trying to recreate the scene of one of the most heavily documented attacks when you decided to interrupt. Perhaps, if you had ventured to research the present situation, you wouldn't have jumped to the wrong conclusions!" Hmph!

4) Mother informs you that the vicar is holding auditions for a concert to raise funds for the church roof and that she thinks you should recite something for him . . . not that you really have much choice in the matter, anyway! Next day, down at the church hall, you're half-way through "The Rime Of The Ancient Mariner" when you notice that what you took to be extreme concentration on the part of the vicar, is actually the sleep of the innocent (AND BORED!). Thus disheartened, there doesn't seem much point in continuing . . . but what DO you do?
a) Sneak out on tiptoes, vowing never to raise the subject of the concert with anyone . . . not even Mother,
b) Cough politely — and loudly — until the vicar wakens and then enquire whether he would like to hear your Shakespeare now, or,
c) Spread your daily tabloid, open at page 3, on the table in front of him before slinking out to inform the Women's Guild Choral Group that the vicar's ready for them!?!

5) You're taking your baby cousin out for a walk in his pram when you decide to nip into the local supermarket for some fruit. You're just looking at some lovely Jaffas when your best mate wanders up. Unfortunately you're so busy talking you forget what you're doing and end up pushing a basket full of oranges instead of a pram. As you approach the checkout, an irate manager rushes up and demands to know where you think you're going with his trolley and why you've left a screaming baby in his fruit and veg. department. What is your reaction?
a) Look at the manager, then at the trolley, back at the manager, then rush off to look for your cousin,
b) Accuse him of bad management for not supplying a creche for shoppers, and also of negligence for causing an obstruction with a trolley full of oranges . . . all the while whispering to your mate to fetch the pram and prepare to dash, or,
c) Calmly tell him that you're merely doing what your auntie asked . . . "Run down to the supermarket and get some oranges for your little cousin." How were you to know it wasn't a special offer? Seemed like a fair swap!

HOW DID YOU SCORE . . .

1) a) 0	b) 5	c) 10
2) a) 0	b) 5	c) 10
3) a) 0	b) 5	c) 10
4) a) 0	b) 5	c) 10
5) a) 0	b) 5	c) 10

Between 0-15

Not very imaginative, are you? You must be everyone's favourite scapegoat. See if you can avoid the blame next time by exercising the little grey bits. You're the world's greatest living stooge . . . but at least your karma's safe!

Between 15-40

You aren't the most quick-witted person around but at least you try. A little bit of fibbing never hurt anyone but your direct approach and your assertiveness could earn you a thump in the ear now and again. "She who fibs and runs away lives to fib another day."

Over 40

Wow! What a whopper-teller! To you, lying is an art form, and you're a master. However, try and restrict your lying to those occasions when you need it. Perhaps a career on the stage would suit you? Remember the story about the boy who cried "Wolf!"? Take heed!

P.S. The part about the canary was a joke, so please don't write in accusing us of being animal haters!

IT'S CHRISTMAS

SHE'S MOVING AWAY

This may sound like a silly problem, but my best friend's moving to the South in the New Year. Although I have got other good friends, Sarah and I have been friends since primary school. We've both said we'll write and see each other during holidays but it won't be the same. I don't know if anything will ever be the same again.

Anita, Newcastle.

I understand how you're feeling just now. I remember how I felt when my friend moved away — I didn't think I'd ever have another friend or I'd ever get over the feeling of loneliness — even though I too had other friends. However, I did, and we still keep in touch and see each other on long weekends and holidays.

You probably feel that you're not going to be able to cope with your friend not being there, but you may just surprise yourself. No doubt your other friends will realise how you feel and be supportive.

Try to go out with them as much as possible. It may seem odd at first without your friend's company, but you'll soon grow used to being with your other friends, even though you'll still miss Sarah.

And, just remember, although you may never have Sarah around, she'll still be there — either on the phone or on a piece of paper.

I WANT TO TELL HER

I'm 17 years old and I've just found out that I'm pregnant. I've decided to have an abortion and I'm now waiting to go into a clinic to have it done. My boyfriend has said he'll stand by me no matter what my decision is. However, although it's all planned out and no-one need ever know, I really feel that I should tell my mum. We're very close and we can talk about things quite easily. Every time we're talking to each other I want to confide in her about what's happening but I just can't. I don't want to worry her — especially since Christmas is coming up. Do you think I should?

Patches Fan, Grampian.

I can undersand the predicament you are in: you know that although you don't need to tell her, you'd like to — after all, she's your friend as well as your mother.

If you tell her now, I don't think that it'll ruin her Christmas. Although she may be a bit shocked to begin with, once she realises that you've taken the positive steps you're taking, and how mature you're being about the situation, she'll be supportive and there for you.

If you don't tell her now and wait till it's over, she'll feel hurt that you couldn't tell her about it and that she couldn't be with you when you needed her most.

A CUT ABOVE

I'd like to do hairdressing when I leave school in the summer but I don't know how to go about it. Can you help?

Mandy, Linlithgow.

You'll probably find that most salons advertise their apprentice or Y.T.S. vacancies in the local newspaper. However, if you keep an eye on the job centre or in touch with your careers office, they'll know about all the Y.T.S. vacancies in your area.

If you'd rather go to college to train as a hairstylist then get in touch with your nearest college of further education who'll give you information about the courses they offer. Good luck!

UNWELCOME COUSINS

My cousins are spending Christmas with us because their parents are going on holiday. I've only ever met them once, a few years ago, and I didn't really like either of them. Not only that, but I'm going to have to give up my bedroom and sleep in my little sister's room so that my cousins can have mine. I was really looking forward to Christmas this year, but it's going to be dreadful with my cousins staying — what can I do? I've told my parents how I feel but they just said I should show some Christmas spirit.

Annie, Workington.

I tend to agree with your parents. Christmas is the time when you should be welcoming and kind to everyone, including your cousins!

As you say, you've only met them once and that isn't really enough time to form a sure opinion of them and, if it was a few years ago, they're bound to have changed. They're probably feeling a bit worried about spending Christmas with you and your family, too, and if you're not very hospitable towards them when they arrive, they're not going to enjoy Christmas either.

So give them a chance. If you make an effort, hopefully you and your cousins will have a wonderful Christmas.

LONELY THIS CHRISTMAS . . .

I was going out with Phil for six months and we were both really fond of each other. However, he finished with me about a month ago leaving me feeling really hurt and lonely. Most of my friends have boyfriends and they're all really happy and have someone to be with while I'm all alone. What can I do? I can see this being a really miserable Christmas for me.

Jennifer, Wolverhampton.

It's always hard getting over someone you were once so fond of, but I can imagine that the desolation and loneliness you feel will be heightened with everyone around you enjoying themselves and urging you to join in.

However, although you may feel that you want to avoid all the Christmas celebrations, make the effort to join in. If you think about it, everyone is more sociable round about the festive period and there are so many parties and dances on, it would be foolish to hide away at home — this could be the medicine you need.

So, look on the positive side of things. Go out with your friends that don't have boyfriends and live it up!

58

— HELP!

It'll soon be Christmas: a time for dances, smooches under the mistletoe and general merriment. But if you've a problem that's worrying you, the thought of Christmas won't be the tonic that it should.

So, we've answered a few of the most common problems sent to us round about this time in an effort to make your Christmas just a little happier.

SHOULD I ASK HIM?

There's this boy who's in the year above me and I've liked him for ages. We often walk home together — he stays quite near me — and we do speak a lot but I don't know if he fancies me. This New Year there's going to be a disco and I thought I would maybe ask him out. I'm scared he says no, which will put the relationship we do have in jeopardy. Do you think I should?

Mary, Inverness.

Yes, I think you should!

It can often be a bit difficult 'testing the water' i.e., working out if he feels the same way as you do. However, if you word what you're going to say carefully it can be ambiguous. Why not ask him in a light-hearted tone if he wants to come with you to the New Year Disco? There's nothing too pushy about that, is there?

If he says yes, be calmly cool about it. Although it's not definite that you'll go out with each other, it's the only way you can approach the situation without causing any embarrassing moments, for either of you.

Good luck!

IS IT TOO LATE?

I've made an awful mess of things. Since we went back to school after the summer holidays I've mucked about and haven't done much work.

My parents got an awful shock when they saw my report card but they've been OK about it. However, I know I've disappointed them. What shall I do? I want to prove to them I can do it but I think it's too late.

Fiona, Glasgow.

Firstly, it's not too late to do something about it. But you have to realise that you'll have to do twice the amount of work during these next few months.

You've learnt the hard way that messing about at school may be more fun than working, but doesn't actually get you anywhere.

Speak to a teacher you can confide in and tell him/her how you feel. If you can prove to them that you really want to work, they'll be more than helpful.

So, do something positive about the situation that you're in. That way, even if you don't do fantastically well in your final exams, at least you know you gave it your best shot.

MARC BOLAN

During his school holidays, Marc Bolan used to help his mum out on her stall at London's Berwick Street Market while his dad was out driving his lorry for a living. Eleven years later, he was earning £30,000 an hour on stage as the leader of T-Rex, the biggest British pop sensation of the early 70's.

In 1969, T-Rex were looking forward to playing big gigs in Inverness, Oban and Fort William for £60 a night . . . between six of them. By 1974, Marc Bolan was spending £1000 a week on clothes, owned an office block in London, was accompanied everywhere by a bodyguard, and had sold 32 million records worldwide. His house in Maida Vale was the site where hundreds of fans kept vigil, twenty-four hours a day, seven days a week.

In 1972, Marc hired a pretty backing vocalist to sing on his American tour. Her name was Gloria Jones and she had already won herself the title "Queen Of Northern Soul" with her original version of "Tainted Love" (later covered by Soft Cell). At the time, Gloria was at the tail end of her marriage and Marc was separated from his wife, June Child. Within a year, romance had blossomed. Marc was devoted to Gloria. For instance, one night, after a gig in Miami, Gloria asked Marc if they could have some seafood. Marc sent his limousine to pick up a restaurant's entire stock of lobster, clams and oysters.

Soon there was cause for an even bigger celebration when Gloria and Marc had a son. Taking his cue from David Bowie's son, Zowie, Marc named him Rolan.

In 1977, Marc was on the road again to take advantage of the punk craze . . . and so were his fans! When a bottle of bubbly, with a love note attached, was hurled through his bedroom window, he merely stated, "I suppose these are the slings and arrows you have to bear if you want to earn an outrageous fortune!". Unfortunately, Marc didn't get a chance to cash in on his continuing success. On September 15, 1977, Gloria's car went out of control, smashed into a tree and, although she was only injured, Marc was killed outright.

It is a strange coincidence that Marc had once told his ex-wife's mother that he would never live to be 30. He was killed just two weeks before his thirtieth birthday. In the months following his death, Marc was honoured in various ways by his adoring fans. He was voted The

World's Best Male Vocalist and The Best Dressed Male Singer Of 1977 in a pop poll; four members of the T-Rex Easy Action Club changed their names by deed poll to Marc Bolan and one girl changed hers to Zinc Alloy, the title of one of his albums; some fans started an appeal to buy a commemorative plaque for his grave and others made pilgrimages to the site of the crash and adorned the tree that the car crashed into with scarves, posters and messages to their idol. In 1981, when it was rumoured that the tree, at Barnes Common, would be chopped down for reasons of road safety, armies of Bolan fans stated that they would take charge of the situation and chop the tree down for souvenirs.

Marc Bolan's influence has spread throughout the spectrum of modern music and it is easy to see the similarities between his fanatical following and that of Bros, Wet Wet Wet, Bon Jovi, etc. Bolan himself was sceptical of people's blind dedication . . . "I think it's sad that so many youngsters live their lives through people like me instead of being themselves!"

IT'S QUITE COMMON FOR POP STARS, FILM STARS AND EVEN DIRECTORS TO MENTION A LONG STREAM OF NAMES WHEN ASKED TO TALK OF THEIR INFLUENCES. MANY OF THEM YOU WILL PROBABLY NEVER HAVE HEARD OF, BUT PATCHES NOW TAKES YOU ON AN EDUCATIONAL TRIP THROUGH THE LIVES OF SOME OF THE BEST KNOWN AND OFT-QUOTED CULT FIGURES OF THE PAST DECADES.

MARILYN MONROE

Marilyn Monroe was born at Los Angeles General Hospital on June 1 1926. The name on her cot was Norma Jean Mortensen and the proud mother was one Gladys Monroe Baker Mortensen. Six months later, Marilyn's grandmother, Della Hogan Monroe Grainger, took her along to be baptised . . . as Norma Jean Baker! An unhappy childhood hit an all-time low in 1935 when, at the age of nine, young Norma Jean was taken into the Los Angeles Orphans' Home Society after her mother suffered a breakdown and was committed to the state asylum in Norwalk.

By the time she reached the age of eleven, Norma Jean had moved in with her Aunt Grace and made a lot of friends in the neighbourhood, not least a handsome young chap called Jim Dougherty. Five years passed and, at the age of sixteen, Norma Jean Baker said yes when 20-year-old Dougherty proposed marriage. During the war years, while Jim was overseas with the Merchant Marines, his wife was making a good living and building an even better reputation as a glamour model on magazine covers . . . a tonic for the troops! However, it also became apparent to both parties that the marriage was in need of something more than a tonic and, in 1946, they split. The same year, Norma Jean landed a contract with 20th Century Fox . . . and became Marilyn Monroe!

Between 1948, when she appeared in her first ever movie, "Scudda Hoo! Scudda Hay!", and 1953, when she starred in her first Monroe movie, "Niagara", Marilyn had been cast in eighteen films, but it was from '53 until '61 that she made herself a legend with title roles in "Gentlemen Prefer Blondes", "How To Marry A Millionaire", "River Of No Return", "There's No Business Like Show Business", "The Seven Year Itch", "Bus Stop", "The Prince And The Showgirl", "Some Like it Hot", "Let's Make Love" and "The Misfits".

Marilyn's second marriage, to baseball hero Joe DiMaggio, was as rocky as her first, and lasted from 1954 to 1955. It was on the set of "The Seven Year Itch", when Marilyn was shooting the classic scene where her dress is blown up by the gust of wind through the subway grating, that Joe realised that she belonged to the world and not just to him.

In 1950, Marilyn had met the playwright Arthur Miller and a warm friendship developed which, in time, turned into romance. They were married in 1956 after Arthur had finalised his own divorce. However, two miscarriages broke Marilyn's heart and soon her third marriage ended. There were other men in Marilyn's life after that, though. Arthur Miller had introduced Marilyn to Yves Montand, and even suggested that he be the male lead her next picture, "Let's Make Love". Marilyn fell for him immediately but, unfortunately for her, he opted to remain with his wife. The most controversial of Marilyn's liasons was with President John F. Kennedy. This was another ill-fated attempt at romance. Marilyn's decision to fly to New York to sing "Happy Birthday" to him at his party resulted in her being fired from what would have been her last movie, "Something's Got To Give". On August 5 1962, Marilyn Monroe was found dead in her bedroom.

There are different opinions as to what actually happened that night. Stories range from those about Marilyn being so depressed she took an overdose, to those claiming that she was murdered by the Mafia, the CIA, the FBI or the Russians for her connection with Kennedy.

Marilyn's appeal was, and still is, universal. She has influenced both males and females since she first appeared in her starring roles and is survived by a whole host of modern day Monroes!

Last word goes to Elton John . . . "Goodbye, Norma Jean!"

JIM MORRISON

James Douglas Morrisson, lead singer of The Doors, always had an air of mystery about him. As a teenager, he read more than he ate and dreamed of following in the footsteps of Arthur Rimbaud, the father of French symbolist poetry, who had written all he had to write by the time he was twenty and became an arms dealer in North Africa. As it turned out, Jim finished high school and enrolled at the School of Cinematography at UCLA. It was here, at the film school which produced a host of renowned directors such as Martin Scorcese, that Jim wrote the lyric that caused The Doors to be opened.

On Venice Beach, just outside LA, Jim met another film student, Ray Manzarek, who asked him what he'd been up to. When Jim replied that he'd been writing some songs, Ray asked if he could hear one of them. After Jim had sung a few verses of "Moonlight Drive", Ray claimed that he had "never heard such wonderful, groovy words to a rock song before." There and then, they decided to "try and crash the music biz." The crash was more of a bang and, after a regular stint at the Whiskey-A-Go-Go in Hollywood, The Doors became recording artists.

Jim Morrison was certainly a rather *enigmatic* personality. On his record company biography he dropped one 's' from his surname and, where it asked for details of other members of his family, he wrote one word: dead. His mother, father, younger brother and sister were, in fact,quite healthy and living on a naval base where his father was later to become an Admiral. He explained to his hairdresser how he wanted his hair cut by producing a picture of Alexander The Great torn from a history book and described it as "like a bird's wing". Once, he had a coat made from the skin of an unborn foal but, when someone mistook it for seal-skin, he took it off, crumpled it up and threw it in an airport trash can. On other occasions he was charged by the police for stealing a policeman's hat from the stage and throwing it into the crowd, attempting to incite a riot, lewd and lascivious behaviour on-stage, and saying the odd naughty word in states where that sort of thing is frowned upon. Eventually, the police were waiting in the wings at every Doors concert with arrest warrants, already filled out with each band-member's name, just waiting to write down which offence they were arresting them for!

In 1971, Jim left the States for Paris where he met his girlfriend, Pamela. It was to be a holiday for both of them and to allow Jim to write. His two volumes of poetry, "The Lords" and "The New Creatures", had just been published and he'd recorded an album of poetry, "The American Prayer", which was to be set to music. Unfortunately, Jim never returned to the USA. He had been coughing blood for almost a month and told some close friends he expected to die soon. He was found dead, from either a heart attack or pneumonia, in the bath at his Paris flat on July 3. He was 27. He was buried in the Poet's Corner at the Père La Chaise

cemetery in Paris, beside Oscar Wilde, Honor de Balzac and Eva Peron and is remembered as Jim Morrison: Poet, 1943-1971.

There is, however, another story. Jim always harboured the fantasy of faking his death and disappearing to Africa. He even went as far as to tell his friends that if he ever did, he would contact them secretly using the name Mr Mojo Risin', an anagram of his own. There is still a mystery about Jim's death because, first of all, the doctor who signed his death certificate cannot be traced, and secondly, the only other person who saw his body was his girlfriend, Pamela. Sadly, her secret, if she had one to tell, went with her to her grave when she died two years later.

Jim Morrison's influence has survived to the present day, even if he hasn't. Morrissey shares his passion for literature, Michael Hutchence of INXS has dressed in the same black leather and a thousand others have copied his lifestyle and stage antics. In an age of synths and samplers, The Doors should be remembered as the first keyboard band.

Jim Morrison could have written his own obituary in any of the lines from his classic, "The End", but his close friend, the poet Michael McLure, said, not long after Jim's death, "I didn't expect Jim to live very long . . . not at the intensity at which he lived. There are worse things than dying." Pamela once said, "He says that his spirit gets so far out of his body he's afraid, one day, it won't be able to come back."

ANDY WARHOL

Andy Warhol is thought to have been born in 1928 of Czechoslovakian parents, with the name Warhola. During his life, he accrued a personal fortune of £28,000,000 — just by observing!

Claiming the attention of the New York world with his acrylic paintings of Campbell's soup tins, he went on to make movies, form one of the most influential underground rock bands of the 60's and become incredibly wealthy. The band was The Velvet Underground and their influence can be heard in bands like Voice Of The Beehive, The House Of Love, Talking Heads and others too numerous to mention.

Warhol studied to be a commercial artist at the Carnegie Institute and his first professional job was drawing shoe designs for a company in New York. Using his natural talent for being 'different', Andy put on an exhibition of shoes, painted gold, and named each exhibit after a film star. It wasn't until 1961, however, that his contribution to the art history books Pop Art, became popular. His system was perfect . . . everything was silk-screened. He didn't even have to paint them himself, he could hire people to do it all for him. He'd already made the transition from artist to entrepreneur. His next step was film.

Andy Warhol movies take a lot of love or stamina to sit through. "Empire" is an eight hour view of the Empire State Building . . . from the same angle. "Kiss" is exactly that, one kiss, which lasts six hours! "Sleep" shows someone sleeping for six hours, "Eat" shows someone eating for six hours and "Haircut" is self-explanatory. "My films," said Warhol, "are just a way of taking up time."

Andy Warhol always had his fair share of critics. Perhaps the *least* voluble was Valerie Solanis, founder and only member of the Society for Cutting Up Men. She is an actress, writer and psychologist but, in 1968 could find no answer to Warhol apart from walking up to him and shooting him three times before giving herself up to the police. Warhol survived and she was sentenced to three years imprisonment.

Famous for two decades for claiming that everyone should be famous for fifteen minutes, Andy Warhol had his last fifteen minutes of fame at St Patrick's Cathedral in New York on April 1 1987 at a special memorial service to commemorate his death on February 23 1987. He was 58.

A MATCH MADE IN HEAVEN?

Do you know where Venus, the planet of love, was on the day you were born? No? We thought not — that's why we've drawn up the great chart on the next page. It will reveal what you're like when you're in love, who you'll be attracted to and, most importantly, who you'll be best suited to . . .

TO USE THE VENUS CHART

Look for the date in our table which comes as near as possible before your birthday and note the number. Follow our key to find out where Venus was when you were born:

1. Aries
2. Taurus
3. Gemini
4. Cancer
5. Leo
6. Virgo
7. Libra
8. Scorpio
9. Sagittarius
10. Capricorn
11. Aquarius
12. Pisces

Example: What is the Venus sign for someone born 16th January, 1973? Look in the table — the first date before the birthday is 11 January, 1973. The number for that date is 10. The corresponding Venus sign in the key is Capricorn.

VENUS IN ARIES

Your heart rules your head so look out for some bumpy times ahead. You love the danger and excitement of blind dates and constantly change boyfriends.

You're not backwards at coming forwards, are you, but you know how to have fun! You enjoy good times and you hate slushy, sentimental stuff and dull routines. Try a Leo if you want a bit of excitement.

VENUS IN TAURUS

You don't jump into things — you like to take your time and charm your way into relationships. To you, your boyfriend has to be your best friend, too.

Good times for you mean good food and long walks in the country. You need a boy who will share your love of nature and want to go steady. Look for Capricorns or Cancerians — they'll suit you best.

VENUS IN GEMINI

You little flirt, you! With Venus in the sign of twins you'll feel happy with two partners at the same time.

You've got the fastest chat up lines on the go and you're great at winding people up. You need a boyfriend who won't be put off by this, or by your two-timing. Try Librans, they'll bring you down to earth.

VENUS IN CANCER

You're shy and cautious, but your charm will win everyone over.

Once you've fallen, the boy in your life will become everything to you and you'll want nothing more than to be his girlfriend.

You're sentimental and affectionate and your guy will need to understand your private moods and not question them. Aquarians leave you uninspired but Taureans and Pisceans are warm and caring.

VENUS IN LEO

Heads turn when you pass by and this can make you vain and conceited.

You need to feel loved because you only come to life when you're in a relationship.

No doubt you'll break a lot of hearts in your search for true love, but once you've found it, you're totally committed. Seek out the signs which appreciate you most, especially Aries.

VENUS IN VIRGO

You're not quick to fall in love, are you? You're seeking an ideal relationship and you can be too much of a perfectionist sometimes. Put some effort into it and attempt to compromise. Put others first for a change and look out for Virgonians.

1973 1974 1975 1976 1977 1978 1979 1980

DATE	NO.	DATE	NO.	DATE	NO.	DATE	NO.	DATE	NO.	DATE	NO.	DATE	NO.	DATE	NO.
11 JAN	10	29 JAN	10	6 JAN	11	1 JAN	9	6 JAN	11	3 JAN	9	4 JAN	12	21 JAN	1
4 FEB	11	28 FEB	11	30 JAN	12	26 JAN	10	30 JAN	12	22 JAN	10	2 FEB	1	14 FEB	12
28 FEB	12	6 APR	12	23 FEB	1	19 FEB	11	23 FEB	1	13 FEB	11	6 JUN	2	10 MAR	1
24 MAR	1	4 MAY	1	19 MAR	2	15 MAR	12	20 MAR	2	12 MAR	12	6 JUL	3	3 APR	2
18 APR	2	31 MAY	2	13 APR	3	8 APR	1	14 APR	3	10 APR	1	3 AUG	4	27 APR	3
12 MAY	3	25 JUN	3	9 MAY	4	2 MAY	2	10 MAY	4	4 MAY	2	29 AUG	5	22 MAY	4
5 JUN	4	21 JUL	4	6 JUN	5	27 MAY	3	6 JUN	5	29 MAY	3	23 SEP	6	16 JUN	5
30 JUN	5	14 AUG	5	9 JUL	6	20 JUN	4	8 JUL	6	17 JUN	4	17 OCT	7	12 JUL	6
25 JUL	6	8 SEP	6	2 SEP	7	14 JUL	5	9 SEP	7	19 JUL	5	10 NOV	8	8 AUG	7
19 AUG	7	2 OCT	7	4 OCT	8	8 AUG	6	1 OCT	8	15 AUG	6	4 DEC	9	7 SEP	8
13 SEP	8	26 OCT	8	9 NOV	9	1 SEP	7	9 NOV	9	1 SEP	7	28 DEC	10	12 OCT	9
9 OCT	9	19 NOV	9	7 DEC	10	26 SEP	8	7 DEC	10	27 SEP	8			21 NOV	10
5 NOV	10	13 DEC	10			20 OCT	9			17 OCT	9				
7 DEC	11					14 NOV	10			21 NOV	10				
						9 DEC	11			3 DEC	11				

VENUS IN LIBRA

Although your relationships come first, you need some time to yourself and with female friends.

Your boyfriend must share your tastes in music and art, as well as your honesty and tact. With your natural distrust of passion and illogical emotions, you'll want to be fair minded and reasonable. Match up with Gemini and you'll be in heaven.

VENUS IN SCORPIO

You demand intense committment — you possess your guy and you're very prone to jealousy. Once you're suspicious, you can brood silently for days. However, you're often the deceitful one — don't be tempted by two-timing!

The calm Cancerian or Piscean will suit you best, but sometimes you need the excitement only a Leo could provide.

VENUS IN SAGITTARIUS

You're a sucker for the tall, dark, handsome, athletic types — you don't ask for much, do you?

You're willing to take a gamble and you need adventure in your life. Your boyfriend needs to be able to take the rough and tumble and, if he gets too serious, run a mile — you don't want to get bogged down with someone too soon. Aquarius and Aries will give you the space you need.

VENUS IN CAPRICORN

To some you seem cold hearted, but really, you're just looking for a serious relationship and you won't waste time with non-starters.

You're very practical, thinking of career before romance and you're quite prepared to wait for the right boy to come along. Once he does, it'll be for good. You're best suited to a quiet Virgonian or a steady Taurean.

VENUS IN AQUARIUS

You're unpredictable — friends are as important as boyfriends. You expect a lot from boyfriends but you might be disappointed.

When you're in love with someone new, you'll still feel for your ex-boyfriends, but don't underestimate how much your new boyfriend likes you! The ones who'll like you best are Librans and Scorpions.

VENUS IN PISCES

You are the most romantic of all the signs. You love anything smoochy or slushy.

You've a vivid imagination and you're always daydreaming of knights on white chargers and handsome princes.

Go for someone who'll share your flights of fancy and won't stunt your dreams. Perhaps a Sagittarian or a Taurean.

THIS IS GOING TO BE MY BEST CHRISTMAS EVER!

ME TOO. I'M REALLY LOOKING FORWARD TO BEING WITH ALISTER.

THE LAST DAY OF TERM! HURRAH! THREE WEEKS OF FREEDOM!

EVERYONE EXCEPT ME HAS GOT PARTIES AND CELEBRATIONS TO LOOK FORWARD TO . . .

Joanne was still very much the new girl at College and, as Christmas approached, she still felt out of things . . .

All I want for Christmas...

ARE YOU COMING INTO TOWN TO DO SOME CHRISTMAS SHOPPING WITH US, TANIA?

ER . . . NO. ALISTER SAID HE'D MEET ME.

LOOKS LIKE HE'S LATE — AS USUAL.

AT LEAST SHE HAS A BOYFRIEND. I HAVEN'T GOT ANYONE.

OH ALISTER'S ALWAYS LATE! I THINK THAT BOYFRIEND OF MINE HASN'T GOT ANY SENSE OF TIME!

I HOPE YOU HAVE A NICE EVENING. SEE YOU LATER.

I FEEL REALLY SORRY FOR TANIA. ALISTER'S GIVING HER A BAD TIME BUT SHE CAN'T SEE IT.

HE ACTUALLY TRIED TO DATE ME LAST WEEK — AND I'M NOT THE FIRST. BUT I COULDN'T TELL TANIA — SHE'S SO KEEN ON HIM.

NO-ONE SEEMS TO BE BOTHERED ABOUT ME. THEY'RE ALL WRAPPED UP IN TANIA'S PROBLEMS. I CAN SEE THIS CHRISTMAS IS GOING TO BE TERRIBLE.

But, a little later, as Joanne was waiting on her bus . . .

HI, JOANNE. HASN'T YOUR BUS COME YET?

I THOUGHT YOU WERE MEETING ALISTER?

WELL, HE WAS LATE TURNING UP, SO I RANG HIS OFFICE. HE'S HAD TO WORK LATE AGAIN.

Joanne felt sorry for Tania, but like Cath, felt she shouldn't interfere . . .

IF YOU'RE AT A LOOSE END OVER CHRISTMAS, YOU CAN ALWAYS RING ME, YOU KNOW.

WELL, HOPEFULLY, I'LL BE SPENDING ALL MY TIME WITH ALISTER! BUT HAVE A NICE CHRISTMAS, WON'T YOU, JOANNE?

And Joanne was alone again . . . with nothing to look forward to.

65

continued on page 68

IT'S SEW EASY!

Introducing Patches exclusive skirt pattern! For an easy-to-make, versatile style, try making this full, gathered skirt. It can all be done on the machine — so you've no boring hand-stitching to worry about! As you can see from our photographs, you can wear it casually during the day, or dress it up for night. It's the perfect addition to every girl's wardrobe. So, don't just sit there, thinking about it, get out your sewing machine, and give it a go — now!

WHAT YOU'LL NEED

1 m. 80 cm. (2 yds.) of 150 cm. (60″) wide fabric or,
3 m. (3¼ yds.) of 115 cm. (45″) wide fabric or,
3 m. (3¼ yds.) of 90 cm. (36″) wide fabric.
1 reel of matching thread.
1 piece of 2 cm. (¾″) wide elastic measuring 1″ LESS than your waist size.

CUTTING OUT

It's easier and safer to cut the pattern pieces out on paper first and pin them onto the fabric, rather than draw the shapes directly onto the fabric.
Fold fabric in two, lengthwise, and cut out as follows:

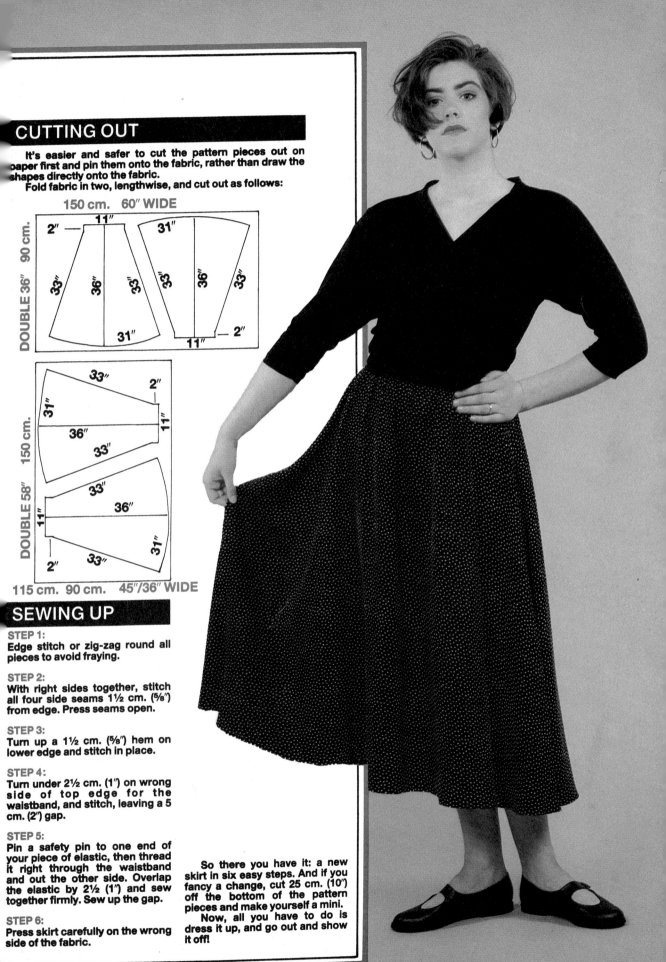

150 cm. 60" WIDE

DOUBLE 36" 90 cm.

2" 11" 31"
33" 36" 33" 33" 36" 33"
31" 2"
11"

DOUBLE 58" 150 cm.

33" 2"
31" 11"
36"
33"
33"
36"
11"
31"
2" 33"

115 cm. 90 cm. 45"/36" WIDE

SEWING UP

STEP 1:
Edge stitch or zig-zag round all pieces to avoid fraying.

STEP 2:
With right sides together, stitch all four side seams 1½ cm. (⅝") from edge. Press seams open.

STEP 3:
Turn up a 1½ cm. (⅝") hem on lower edge and stitch in place.

STEP 4:
Turn under 2½ cm. (1") on wrong side of top edge for the waistband, and stitch, leaving a 5 cm. (2") gap.

STEP 5:
Pin a safety pin to one end of your piece of elastic, then thread it right through the waistband and out the other side. Overlap the elastic by 2½ (1") and sew together firmly. Sew up the gap.

STEP 6:
Press skirt carefully on the wrong side of the fabric.

So there you have it: a new skirt in six easy steps. And if you fancy a change, cut 25 cm. (10") off the bottom of the pattern pieces and make yourself a mini.
Now, all you have to do is dress it up, and go out and show it off!

But next day, there was an unexpected confrontation with — Alister!

HEY, GET DOWN, YOU MANIAC POOCH! YOU'LL MAKE ME DROP EVERYTHING!

OH, ALISTER! I'M SO SORRY. REX, GET DOWN, YOU BAD BOY!

I'M REALLY SORRY, ALISTER. I HOPE THERE ISN'T ANY DAMAGE.

DON'T WORRY, THERE'S NOTHING BREAKABLE IN THERE. BESIDES, I'VE WANTED A CHANCE TO SAY HELLO, AND WELCOME TO TOWN.

OH, THANKS, ALISTER. I'D LIKE TO COME OUT WITH YOU AND TANIA SOME TIME . . .

I DON'T SUPPOSE YOU'VE BEEN HERE LONG ENOUGH TO FIND YOUR WAY ROUND TOWN. ANY TIME YOU NEED AN ESCORT, I'D BE GLAD TO HELP OUT.

His next words stunned her . . .

I DIDN'T MEAN TANIA AND ME. I MEANT JUST YOU AND ME. ON OUR OWN. I'VE BEEN WANTING TO GET TO KNOW YOU EVER SINCE I FIRST MET YOU.

OH, ALISTER! YOU CAN'T MEAN THAT! I MEAN . . . YOU'RE GOING OUT WITH TANIA!

ACTUALLY, I WON'T BE GOING OUT WITH TANIA FOR MUCH LONGER, JOANNE. I'VE BEEN TRYING TO FIND THE COURAGE TO BREAK IT OFF FOR SOME TIME . . .

OH . . . I SEE.

It explained why Tania was having problems with Alister . . .

IN THAT CASE, I'LL FINISH IT STRAIGHT AWAY. I DON'T WANT TO LOSE YOU, JOANNE . . .

I COULDN'T POSSIBLY GO OUT WITH YOU IF YOU WERE STILL DATING TANIA. IT WOULDN'T BE FAIR.

I CAN'T BELIEVE THIS! HE'S LIKED ME FOR AGES!

Things had suddenly taken a turn for the better . . .

I JUST HOPE TANIA UNDERSTANDS. I COULDN'T GO OUT WITH ALISTER BEHIND HER BACK . . .

BUT IF HE'S PREPARED TO BREAK WITH TANIA, THERE'S NO REASON WHY I SHOULDN'T GO OUT WITH HIM! AFTER ALL, WE LIKE EACH OTHER, AND WE'RE BOTH FREE . . .

68

The next day, Joanne was already making plans for her date with Alister . . .

I'M SILLY TO DOUBT WHAT HE SAID! IF HE REALLY LIKES ME, HE'LL FINISH WITH TANIA, AND EVERYTHING WILL WORK OUT . . .

HI, JOANNE. LOOKING FOR A NEW DRESS?

But seeing Tania, she felt a flood of guilt . . .

OH, HI, TANIA. HOW ARE THINGS?

OH, JUST ABOUT THE SAME. I WAS HOPING TO GO TO JUNE'S PARTY WITH ALISTER LAST NIGHT, BUT HE COULDN'T MAKE IT AGAIN.

SO YOU DIDN'T SEE HIM AT ALL LAST NIGHT? HE DIDN'T SAY ANYTHING TO YOU?

WELL, HE MADE ANOTHER DATE FOR TONIGHT. SAID HE'D DEFINITELY BE THERE AND THAT HE WAS LOOKING FORWARD TO SEEING ME!

Joanne was suddenly uncertain . . .

WELL, I HOPE EVERYTHING'S ALL RIGHT THIS EVENING . . .

SO DO I! I WANT TO TALK THINGS OVER WITH ALISTER AND FIND OUT FOR CERTAIN WHERE I STAND.

And Joanne couldn't help feeling doubtful about Alister . . .

She couldn't help remembering that Alister had tried to date Cath a few weeks ago . . .

BUT THAT WAS BEFORE HE MET ME! I'M SURE HE MEANT WHAT HE SAID TO ME. AND YET . . . I CAN'T BE SURE UNTIL HE'S REALLY FINISHED WITH TANIA . . .

Despite her doubts, she couldn't help the little flutter of joy when she unexpectedly met Alister . . .

HI THERE! IT'S GREAT TO SEE YOU AGAIN!

OH, ALISTER! I THOUGHT YOU WERE GOING TO TELL TANIA LAST NIGHT.

I WOULD HAVE TOLD HER, JOANNE, BUT WE HAD TO WORK LATE DUE TO THE CHRISTMAS RUSH. I PROMISE THAT I'LL TELL HER TONIGHT, THOUGH.

WELL . . . AS LONG AS YOU'RE SURE, ALISTER.

But Joanne still felt uncertain . . .

I'M SUPPOSED TO BE MEETING ALISTER TONIGHT, BUT I CAN'T GO IF HE HASN'T BROKEN WITH TANIA. IT JUST WOULDN'T BE FAIR . . .

She didn't know what to think when Tania herself turned up a while later . . .

OH, JOANNE, I'M SORRY TO BURST IN LIKE THIS, BUT I HAD TO TELL SOMEONE. IT'S ALL OVER. I'M THROUGH WITH ALISTER.

YOU MEAN . . . IT'S FINISHED? HE'S REALLY BROKEN WITH YOU?

SO IT'S OVER! HE'S TOLD HER! THAT MEANS HE'S KEPT HIS WORD TO ME, AND HE'S FREE!

I TOLD HIM IT WAS OVER LAST NIGHT. THE MOMENT I FOUND OUT HE'D BEEN GOING OUT WITH CHRISTINE BAKER FOR WEEKS BEHIND MY BACK.

CHRISTINE BAKER? YOU MEAN HE'S BEEN TWO-TIMING YOU . . . WITH . . . CHRISTINE . . .?

I'D SUSPECTED THERE WAS SOMEONE ELSE, JOANNE, AND AT LAST I CAUGHT THEM TOGETHER! HE'S BEEN LYING TO ME FOR WEEKS — THE RAT.

69

continued over

I THINK THERE HAVE BEEN OTHERS TOO. CATH HAS DROPPED HINTS ABOUT HIM. I DIDN'T WANT TO KNOW. OH, JOANNE, I'M BETTER OFF WITHOUT HIM.

THERE'S SOMETHING I THINK YOU OUGHT TO KNOW, TANIA . . . I DON'T KNOW HOW TO TELL YOU THIS, BUT ALISTER ASKED ME OUT TOO. HE TOLD ME THAT YOU TWO HAD SPLIT UP WEEKS AGO . . .

I'M REALLY SORRY, TANIA, BUT I COULDN'T KEEP IT TO MYSELF ANY LONGER. WE'RE FRIENDS AND I DON'T THINK THAT A RAT LIKE ALISTER SHOULD BREAK US UP.

I DON'T BLAME YOU, JOANNE, HONESTLY. I SHOULD HAVE REALISED A LONG TIME AGO THAT THINGS WEREN'T RIGHT BETWEEN ME AND ALISTER . . . HE JUST MEANT SO MUCH TO ME THAT I COULDN'T SEE IT.

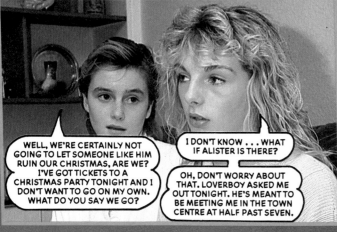

WELL, WE'RE CERTAINLY NOT GOING TO LET SOMEONE LIKE HIM RUIN OUR CHRISTMAS, ARE WE? I'VE GOT TICKETS TO A CHRISTMAS PARTY TONIGHT AND I DON'T WANT TO GO ON MY OWN. WHAT DO YOU SAY WE GO?

I DON'T KNOW . . . WHAT IF ALISTER IS THERE?

OH, DON'T WORRY ABOUT THAT. LOVERBOY ASKED ME OUT TONIGHT. HE'S MEANT TO BE MEETING ME IN THE TOWN CENTRE AT HALF PAST SEVEN.

WHICH GIVES ME AN ABSOLUTELY BRILLIANT IDEA . . . C'MON, TANIA, GO HOME AND GET YOUR VERY BEST GLAD RAGS ON. WE'RE GOING TO TEACH ALISTER A LESSON HE WON'T FORGET!

If Alister had known what was about to happen he wouldn't have been quite so impatient . . .

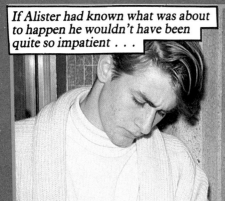

And . . .

OH, HELLO, ALISTER. YOU'RE STANDING THERE LIKE YOU'VE BEEN STOOD UP OR SOMETHING. WHAT DO YOU THINK, TANIA?

THAT IT COULDN'T HAPPEN TO A NICER PERSON! C'MON, WHAT ARE WE WAITING FOR — LET'S GO TO THE DISCO.

IT WAS JUST LUCK THAT MY NEXT-DOOR-NEIGHBOUR AND HIS MATE WERE GOING TO THE DISCO TOO, BUT ALISTER DOESN'T KNOW THAT . . . HE LOOKS LIKE SOMEONE'S STOLEN HIS CHRISTMAS STOCKING OR SOMETHING.

70

WELL, MAYBE HE'LL UNDERSTAND HOW WE FEEL NOW. I ONLY WISH IT HADN'T ALL WORKED OUT LIKE THIS . . . I HAVE A FEELING THAT ALISTER COULD HAVE MADE THIS A CHRISTMAS TO REMEMBER . . .

THE END

DO YOU HAVE STAR QUALITY?

Would you like to have a limo waiting outside your penthouse for you? Posters of you on every teenager's wall? Mountains of fan mail waiting to be answered?

If you dream about having your name in the gossip columns, try our quiz — and see if you've got what it takes . . .!

1) How do you spend your Saturdays?
a. You rise at lunchtime, slob around all afternoon — still in your nightie — playing with the cat, munching crisps and watching an old black and white movie on the box with the sound down while you shoogle about and sing along with your sister's Beatles records.
b. Up in time to help Mum with the shopping, make lunch for the family, clean out and wash Dad's car and then tidy your bedroom.
c. Awake by nine o'clock, carefully dressed and fully made-up by lunchtime and then off for the day to elegantly swan round the Virgin megastore in the hope that someone thinks you're a star and pleads for your autograph.

2) The doorbell rings when you're not expecting it to. What do you do?
a. Leave it for someone else to answer.
c. Hastily don an extra layer of Fuchsia lippy, fluff up your Carmen waved locks and then calmly open the door with a glitzy smile on your face — in case it's the Press of course!
b. You slip your tootsies into your knitted slippers and happily pad towards the door, opening it welcomingly, for you know it's Mrs Grouble from next door come for her daily dose of gossip and shortbread.

3) It's your friend's birthday. What do you give her?
c. A signed black and white photograph of yourself.
b. One of those foot spas which are like mini Jacuzzis. You know she'll appreciate it because, like yourself, she's got bad circulation.
a. A box of chocolates, still in the paper bag the shop assistant put it in. You'd have bought her something more exciting but you couldn't decide what she'd like.

4) The Drama Club are holding auditions for the school production of "Hamlet". What part would you go for?
c. Ophelia — you can identify with such a beautiful yet tragic figure.
a. The grave digger. He's only got one scene and a few lines to do so it shouldn't be too much like hard work. And nobody will recognise you on the night because you'll have so much theatrical muck on your face.
b. You wouldn't audition. No, you'd much rather make the costumes, especially since the sewing department have now got those super new Pfaff sewing machines.

5) What are the most essential items in your handbag?
c. A mirror, eyelash curlers, hairspray, eau de cologne, a spare black stocking, vitamin pills . . .
a. Handbag? You carry everything you need in your pouches.
b. That handy knitting gauge you got free from your mother's My Weekly a few years back.

6) If you could meet anyone in the world, who would it be?
a. Tom Cruise — cor, he's a hunk and a half!
b. Delia Smith. She might tell you the secret of perfect puff pastry.
c. Big Buck Dollastein, head of Sparkleland Productions. Then there would be nothing stopping you getting into films, would there?

HOW DID YOU SCORE?

Mostly a's

You're such a lazy slob, it's doubtful you'll ever make it big in any field never mind films. However, the fact that you're such a sloth could be due to two reasons; either you were born idle or it could be your hormones. But, whatever your excuse, just remember the old Malaysian saying, "the slower the slug, the more likely he is to be trampled on".

Mostly b's

Not only are you the most boring person of your age but the only highlight forecast in your life is winning the 1992 Church Fête first prize for rhubarb and ginger jam. Nope, it doesn't look like you'll ever have your name in lights!

Mostly c's

You've got it! Your future seems as bright as a Cambridge honours graduate. However, unless you've got some talent, any fame you do experience won't be long-standing. So, consider some other career, or your mum will be the only person who remembers your birthday!

71

AS TIME GOES BY

THE FASHIONS OF TODAY ARE STILL GREATLY INFLUENCED BY THE STYLES OF THE PAST . . . DON'T BELIEVE US? WELL, TAKE A LOOK AT SOME OF THE OLD FAVOURITES THAT ARE STILL VERY MUCH WITH US NOW.

1) HOLLYWOOD GLAMOUR

This is the real movie-star look, inspired by the likes of Audrey Hepburn in the late 1950's. Ski pants, halter-neck tops and flat pumps are essential for this style. Add a wide elasticated belt, a printed scarf and sunglasses for true authenticity. Perfect for the star-struck among you!

72

2) ICE-COOL ELEGANCE

Wide-legged trousers first became popular in the 1920's, then resurfaced in the 1950's, worn by such stars as Grace Kelly, Rita Hayworth and Katherine Hepburn. Teamed up with a plain white shirt, a chiffon scarf and low-heeled shoes, it can give a masculine style real femininity.

3) SWINGING STYLE

The mini-skirt, one of fashion's most radical discoveries, arrived in the 1960's, died out in the mid 1970's and bounced back again in the late 1980's. It now looks like it's here to stay, to the dismay of many women and the delight of many men. For a truly zany look, wear it with thigh-high boots and a dazzling smile. Only for Brigitte Bardot or the very brave!

) COUNTRY GIRL

Jeans must be the greatest fashion survivor of all. Originally worn as working clothes by farmers, they soon became popularised by movie idols in the 1950's. Since then, they have been an essential in every young person's wardrobe, and sales of denims have recently flourished thanks to a series of advertisements featuring good-looking people and great sounding music. Jeans can be worn anywhere with anything, and they'll see you through a hundred different fashion phases.

PUPPY LOVE

FOR MANY OF YOU, THE BEST PRESENT YOU COULD GET THIS CHRISTMAS WOULD BE A CUTE, CUDDLY LITTLE BALL OF FUN — NAMELY, A PUPPY. FAIR ENOUGH, BUT PUPPIES AREN'T PUPPIES FOR EVER. VERY SOON, YOUR CUTE, CUDDLY LITTLE BALL OF FUN WILL BECOME AN ADULT DOG, NEEDING LOTS OF FOOD, EXERCISE AND, MOST OF ALL, LOVE. SO, WHEN YOUR PUPPY STOPS BEING CUTE AND STARTS NEEDING A LOT OF ATTENTION, WILL YOU BE UP TO THE CHALLENGE? AN AWFUL LOT OF PEOPLE AREN'T, SOMETHING WE FOUND OUT WHEN WE VISITED A TYPICAL COUNCIL KENNELS, AND SAW WHAT HAPPENS TO YOUR UNWANTED PRESENTS.

These are some of the thousands of dogs that are either handed in to the kennels, or found wandering the streets by the kennels' two dog wardens. Once the dogs have been taken into the kennels, the system is this: they are kept for seven days, then put on sale to the public for a few days. If they are still not claimed, the dogs are put to sleep — a nice phrase for a pretty nasty job — one that has to be done by one of the dog wardens, as they are the only ones authorised by the police to carry out the heartbreaking task.

The sad fact is this — if a dog is cute and appealing, it dramatically increases its chances of survival. If a dog has long since left its puppy days behind it, or happens to look a bit scruffy, its fate is pretty much sealed. You may think it's quite cruel to destroy these dogs, when they're perfectly healthy, but there simply isn't the room to house all the unwanted dogs — when you learn that, over the course of the past 10 years, something in the region of 20,000 dogs have been handled BY THIS KENNEL ALONE, you'll see the problems that the kennel workers face.

When you first enter the kennels, the first thing that hits you is the noise — a truly deafening blast of barking and howling. The second thing you notice is the smell — no, these places are not very pleasant at all — concrete walls, iron bars and disinfectant . . . you could be in a prison, but the difference is that these inmates have committed no crimes.

You DO begin to wonder what makes the kennel workers' jobs worthwhile, but you've only got to see what happens when a stray dog is reunited with its owner, to see that the job does have its happy moments. While we were there, a beautiful Doberman was collected by its master. The dog nearly wagged his tail off!
It is really upsetting,

however, is that one in every two dogs that goes into the kennels doesn't come out. It's the wardens' job to go out in the vans and cruise around looking for strays. We were invited by Marion, one of the wardens, to go out with her in the van and see just what her job entails.
After driving around for about an hour, we spotted a dog which didn't seem to belong to anyone, and wasn't wearing a collar. Marion explained that the dogs can be very dangerous sometimes (she has been bitten several times) and you have to be very careful when you try to catch them.
This dog seemed to be quite quiet, but wasn't too happy about being put in the back of the van. Marion always makes sure that the dog is securely tied up, so it won't be hurt on the way to the kennels by the van rocking about. As you can imagine, if you have five or six angry dogs in the back of a small van, things can get a bit rowdy!
Once we got back to the kennels, the dog is put into a pen, and given food and water, then Marion has to write a report of the dog's "capture" — where it was caught; when; if it had a collar on or not and a

description of the dog — in this case, a small, tan-coloured mongrel bitch.
Like all the rest, this dog will be kept for seven days, then put on sale. She may be lucky, however, because she's still quite young and is very attractive.

Obviously, even after reading this, many of you will still get a dog for Christmas. Just remember that the majority of dogs that are picked up during the year are done so just after the festive season. Some have been badly abused, or just left out in the street to fend for themselves, and if that happens, you've read what comes next. All that Marion and her colleagues are saying is this: think carefully before you get a dog as a present — will you have the time to take it for the walks it'll need? Will your mum and dad be able to afford all the food that it will need, and finally, will you still want it when it's not so cute and cuddly any more?

As Marion says, dogs are meant to be man's best friend . . . if we treat our best friends like this, who needs enemies?

SMOOCHY, SMOOCHY...

The ever intrepid Patches reporters ventured out one morning in the search of answers — honest ones. The question . . . WHO WOULD YOU LIKE TO KISS UNDER THE MISTLETOE? . . . The possibilities . . . endless! The answers . . . read on!

1) Kirsty, 15.
"I don't like all the real hunks — I'd love to kiss Craig from Bros. I just hope he sees this!"

2) Davie, "mature".
"Oh, I'd have to say my wife — she's the only woman I've ever wanted to kiss." Aww, isn't that nice!?

3) Neil, 19.
"Um . . . I dunno — ah! Linda Lusardi! Oh, d'you want me to say something romantic? Oh, all right then — my girlfriend — is that OK?"

4) Grant, 20.
"Liz Fraser (dodgy warbler in the Cocteau Twins). She's gorgeous . . . If her lips were busy though it'd be Madonna — she's nice — oh — don't print that, you'll ruin my street cred!" Tough luck, Grant!!

Fiona Stewart, 18.
"Mmm, let me think, Nick Kamen, but I'd close my ears, his singing's awful!"

David, 17.
"I go for sexy women and the sexiest are Cat (Prince's dancer) and Sheila E. Ooh, I can just imagine kissing them . . ."

We leave him babbling as we talk to;

Carolynne, 17.
"I know almost everyone thinks Prince is ugly, but I really like him and Matt Dillon, cor!!"

6) David Dalí (?), 24.
"Being a street artist I look for beauty and art in everything. I'm a perfectionist so it would need to be Kathleen Turner I kissed. She's what I call perfect!"

7) Angela, 16.
"Ooh, I have to say my boyfriend I suppose, but I really fancy Patrick Swayze!"

Cara, 16½.
"I fancy Matt Goss or a guy called Stuzzy." We were left puzzled as she ran off giggling!

8) Roderick, 9.
"My mum. Hee, hee, hee!" We all sighed an 'Awww' while Roderick's mum swelled with pride. He'll get slagged at school for this!

9) Adele, 13.
"Ooh, Matt Goss."

Michelle, 12.
"Matt Goss, he's lovely."

Brian, 13.
"I quite like Kylie Minogue, but don't tell anyone!"

Adele and Michelle also inform us that they'd secretly like to kiss Brian, but hurriedly denied it saying they'd never buy Patches again if we printed it. Well, tough luck, blackmail doesn't work on us, matey!!

10) Lewis, 16.
"I'll be boring and say Debbie Gibson. I really fancy her — and my phone number's . . ."

Kevin, 16.
"I'll be REALLY boring and say Debbie Gibson as well. She's already got my phone number, though!"

OBSESSION!

It's hard to believe it when you read about someone else being obsessed by something or someone. But what happens when that person is you — and there's nothing you can do about it . . . ?

SHARON'S STORY . . .

"FOR six months of my life, I was totally obsessed with Bros. The first time I saw them they were performing "When Will I Be Famous?" on Top Of The Pops. I just couldn't take my eyes off of them. They were so different to anything else around then. They looked fabulous in their ripped Levis, Doc Martens and leather jackets, and their music really lifted me up. My friends, Sarah and Tracey, liked Luke and Matt but when I saw Craig, who played the bass guitar, smile, my whole world changed.

"Craig wasn't like the other two. He had a quiet, sincere personality without the dazzling sureness the twins had. Craig was more on my level and, unlike Luke and Matt, he seemed so real and so close, even though he was far away. I knew from that moment onwards that this was the real thing — this was love. If only I could get to meet Craig, I know he'd like me and, who knows, he might even fall in love with me, too!

"My brothers used to tease me about Craig, but it didn't bother me. I'd just go into my room which was covered in Bros posters, and dream of the day when Craig and I would be together. I joined the fan club and spent a fortune on badges, T-shirts and photographs.

"My whole life revolved around Craig. I'd wake in the morning for school and play my records while I got ready. It was quite hard to concentrate during class because I just couldn't help myself daydreaming about Craig and I being together. I'd often write letters to Craig during classes but all I ever got back was a letter which was obviously photo-copied saying thanks for my letter. I could understand why Craig didn't reply — he'd been quite busy since they were so popular. At night I'd sit in and listen to my Bros records and dream about the day when we'd meet each other; what I'd be wearing, what I'd say to him and what he'd say to me. I'd lie on my bed for hours trying to work out how I could meet him.

"Then I found out Bros were touring Britain. I was overjoyed, but when I asked my mum if I could go and see them she said no, saying that I was too young. No matter how much I screamed and shouted and pleaded she just stuck to her guns. She obviously didn't realise just how much I loved Craig and how this was my big chance to meet him.

"However, with the help of my friend, Sarah, we devised this plan to go and see Bros. We bought the tickets (I'd now used up all my savings buying them as well as all the stuff I'd bought from the fan club), and planned to tell our parents we were staying at each other's overnight.

"When the day of the concert came I was sick with excitement all day. I was so nervous I could hardly speak. But, after the dreadful support act, when Bros came on I've never been so elated in my life. And there he was — he looked absolutely gorgeous and when I jumped up and down and screamed his name I could have sworn he smiled in my direction. We were only a few feet apart, and I remember stretching out to try to touch him.

"I can't remember much else about the concert except that I jumped and screamed so much that I was exhausted, but still excited. When the concert ended I rushed round to the stage door — along with a thousand other fans — to wait for Craig coming out. But this man, who looked like one of the roadies, told us they'd slipped out early. I was devasted. This had been my big chance to meet Craig, and he'd gone. I felt so hurt, so let down, that I just started crying, my heart bursting with painful sobs. After a while I made my way back inside as I'd left Sarah and my jacket behind, but I couldn't find either of them. And then I remembered, my ticket to get home was in my jacket pocket. Unable to control my tears I stumbled about the empty seats looking for my jacket until one of the bouncers asked what was wrong. I spilled it all out and I can remember listening to my own voice and thinking just how silly I must sound. Just then Sarah appeared, she looked as though she'd been crying too. Anyway, unknown to us, the bouncers had got

hold of one of the crowd policemen who said he could help us, then asked for our parents' phone numbers. I was sure Mum and Dad would kill me when they found out what I'd done. When I phoned, Dad was livid but he agreed to pick me up. The wait in the police station was dreadful. I was so scared, cold, hungry but most of all I regretted what I'd done. My dad said nothing to me or Sarah on the way home but when we got back, Mum went spare. And, although I was sorry about what had happened, I never realised how selfish I'd been or how hurt my mum was. When my mum started crying, I felt so guilty — I'd broken her trust in me and deliberately gone against her.

"After that night Craig Logan didn't seem so important any more, even though I still feel a bit gooey when I see pictures of him. And now I'm sort of going out with this boy in the year above me and there is so much in my life, not just someone whom I'd never met or was likely to meet. Real life is so much better."

LOOK JUST FLAB-ULOUS!

Everyone goes on about it, it's meant to be good for you, you can't open a magazine without some idiot wittering on about its delights . . . What is it? *Dieting*, of course! We looked at it from a slightly different point of view . . .

10 REASONS NOT TO DIET!!

1. OK. Think of the long, cold winter nights, snow gently falling outside, and all you're allowed to eat is a lettuce leaf. Wouldn't a hot chocolate and a Hob Nob biscuit be a lot nicer . . . ?

2. There's bound to be some guy out there who prefers the "cuddly" type . . .

3. Imagine all the money you'll save on diet drinks and low fat crisps and have to spend on new clothes that'll fit! It's enough to make your purse have a heart attack . . .

4. What if HE asks you out to dinner and you have to refuse because he'll think you're daft, making a bowl of noodle soup last all night . . .

5. Picture the scene — you're alone with him, in the sitting room, watching "Endless Love", and he whispers something romantic in your ear. In reply . . . your stomach rumbles (you've only had raw carrots and a Diet Coke all day). Could be more than a tad embarrassing, eh?

6. Marilyn Monroe, Diana Dors and Jayne Mansfield were a good couple of stones overweight and *they* were sex symbols, so why shouldn't *you* be?

7. If you were stranded on a desert island, you'd last longer than your skinny pal, wouldn't you, 'cos you've got more fat to burn . . . ? What d'you mean that's pretty far-fetched? We can all dream, can't we?

8. If you went on a diet, you'd have to do some exercises, but the medical profession now say that aerobics does damage to your joints, running ruins your cartilages, you could be run down by a car when cycling, and you could drown swimming, etc . . . Need I say more?

9. You don't have to worry your head with all that stuff about artificial sweetener supposedly causing harm . . .

10. Finally, if people can't like you for what you are, fat *or* skinny, then they sure ain't worth having as friends! (And that's our considered verdict!)

MANDY was totally obsessed but not with a person. Mandy was obsessed by food and it came close to killing her . . .

"It all started when I was about fifteen and my parents sent me to boarding school. I really hated it because they made me board there when, really, I lived close enough to travel.

"However, it would have meant a long train journey every day and my mum would have had to drive me seven miles to the station and back every day, so they decided I should board.

"I was very unhappy at school, missing home and my parents and my horse, but eventually, I made friends with a girl in my year. Her name was Shelley and she was very fat, so when she decided to go on a diet, I said I'd join her to give moral support.

"I wasn't thin but I wasn't fat, either. I'd say I was about 9¾ stones then, which wasn't bad for my height of 5' 6".

"Shelley's diet lasted two weeks, but I was determined to stay on mine,

MANDY'S STORY . . .

hoping that when she saw me getting thinner, she'd start dieting again too.

"I had decided at the beginning that I would need a very strict diet, so I cut out everything except fruit, carrots and black coffee with (meatless) salads every now and then.

"I knew that I was eating far too little by the headaches and dizziness I was having but, after a while, I quite enjoyed feeling ill because it proved I had so much will-power, I could deny my body food even when it was crying out for it.

"I weighed myself every day and, by the time I went home for the holidays, I weighed just under 8½ stone. My mum said I looked great and wasn't I glad I'd lost all that weight?

"I wasn't, though — I still thought I was fat, so I hardly ate at all during the holidays; just apples, salads and coffee, really. I didn't usually eat with the family anyway, so no-one noticed I was starving myself.

"My headaches and dizziness had gone by now but I did notice I wasn't quite as strong as I had been before. I

was having problems controlling my horse and was finding it really difficult to move feed sacks and jumps around the stable and field. I didn't mind, though, because I was getting thinner all the time and that was all that mattered.

"By the time the next school holidays came around, I was under 7 stones and my periods had stopped. Mum was really worried. She tricked me in to going to the doctor by pretending she was ill and asking me to go with her.

"The doctor gave me a week to put on weight and kept warning me about how my health would suffer, but I was convinced everyone was over-reacting and being really stupid. After all, I was in control, what was there to worry about?

"Anyway, to cut a (very) long story short, I ended up in hospital, on a drip, which fed nutrients and glucose in to my body. All the anorexics were weighed every day, but I soon learned how to hide cutlery in my underwear to make me heavier.

"The nurses tried every day to make me eat but the sight of food now made me feel physically sick. My parents threatened to sell my horse if I didn't start eating — I didn't care. What had once been the most important thing in the world to me, now came second to my obsession with my weight.

"My parents did sell my horse and I got worse. I was now 6½ stones and very ill. However, one day I suddenly decided that I couldn't stand to stay in hospital and I was going to eat again to get out. After all, I could always diet again at home.

"So, I did. I wouldn't eat 'normal' food — just salads and fruit — but very slowly I started to put weight on again, and one day, when I reached 9 stones, they told me I could go home. I thought I was obese.

"Of course, once I got home, I started starving myself again but I always went on a binge before my out-patient visits, so I could persuade the doctors I was 'cured'. At last, about eight months later, they told me I didn't have to go back.

"All the time I was in hospital, I'd been studying hard for exams (it was the only way I could get any peace from the nurses) so I now left school and took a job away from home.

"I was working with horses and, as the work was hard and the hours were long, there wasn't much time for eating, so it was easy to starve myself.

"And, eventually, the whole thing would have got totally out of hand again if it hadn't been for my boss, who noticed I was getting too weak to do my job.

"She told me she knew what was going on and that if I didn't start to eat and get my strength back, she would have to sack me.

"So, I had no choice but to eat and, eventually, I realised just how silly I'd been.

"It's taken me over three years to come to my senses and, even now, I feel guilty about eating too much, not to mention feeling obese if I put on even three or four pounds.

"I'll never be totally 'cured' but I'm out of danger, and for most anorexics, that's the best they can hope for."

OBSESSION!

SAMANTHA'S STORY...

"IT was really all my cousin's fault — at least, that's my story and I'm sticking to it! What happened was, one day she persuaded me to go down to the little carnival that comes to our town every summer. I was quite happy to go along, and that night we got chatting to some of the boys that worked on the Waltzer. They were all nice, but there were none I particularly fancied. It was pretty obvious to me, though, that one of the boys, Nathan, was interested in my cousin Nancy, and so we found ourselves spending most evenings down at the carnival.

"Finally Nathan and Nancy started going out together, and they often came up to my house at night to listen to records. We all got on really well — Nathan and I became good friends.

"At the end of the summer, the carnival went away. Nancy was broken hearted, and she lived for Thursday nights when Nathan phoned her. But in February the phone calls stopped, and, when the carnival came back in April, Nathan wouldn't even speak to Nancy.

"For the first two or three weeks I seemed to spend my life dragging Nathan away to ask him what was going on, and it soon became apparent that he was pretty mixed up. He said he felt so bad when he'd had to leave Nancy last year that he was making sure he never got hurt like that again. During that time we became like brother and sister — if we ever needed anyone to talk to we would go to each other. In the end, they did go back out, but Nathan had changed — he treated Nancy like dirt and often dated other girls — not even behind her back! The last straw came when we were all at a friend's 18th and he got off with another girl right in front of Nancy.

"Just about that time, Nathan's aunt, who owns the carnival, asked Nancy and me if we would help out working on her stalls in the school holidays. Of course, we were only too pleased, so our connections with the carnival didn't end there. Nancy got over Nathan quite quickly, and, remarkably, they remained good friends.

"It was then that I started to become fonder and fonder of Nathan. Nancy knew how I felt and just laughed — she's very independent, and she wouldn't have taken him back if he'd begged her. So knowing that Nancy didn't mind, I had a clear field.

"Things carried on as normal —

the three of us worked together all day, then we went up to my house at night. If for some reason Nathan didn't turn up, I would stamp around in a foul mood, practically in tears. I suppose I should have noticed then that this wasn't right, but I didn't.

"By this time, Nathan was beginning to suspect that I fancied him, and he likes a challenge. I got off with him a couple of times, and that sealed my fate! I was determined I wasn't going to get

involved, but it was too late for that. He dropped me like a week-old fish and started seeing other girls. I was practically suicidal every time he found a new one, in case he liked her and stayed with her, but he never did.

"As the end of the summer came closer, the thought of Nathan going away out of my reach started to get too much to bear. Thinking about him travelling round the country, meeting other girls and forgetting about me drove me crazy. For a while, I couldn't think what to do, but desperation gave me a good idea. I asked Nathan's aunt if she needed any help in the other places they went to, maybe at weekends or holidays. To my delight she said yes, that was just what she could do with.

"To cut a long story short, I left school (I was seventeen) to the complete fury of my parents, signed on the dole, this being a couple of years ago, and when the carnival left in August, I left with it.

"Nathan's aunt worked me hard, but she was good to me. I grew very fond of her and her husband. They were a bit over protective, though — I wasn't allowed out unless one of the boys went with me — not even up to the phone. But I was happy. I was close to Nathan, and I knew what he was doing.

"I travelled with them for about a year and a half, happy when Nathan was nice to me, depressed when he wasn't. I always held out some hope that Nathan would see the error of his ways and decide I was the best thing that ever happened to him. Even when he got a steady girlfriend I wasn't discouraged, because she treated him badly, and it was always me he came to for sympathy. I tried to do everything for him — washing his clothes, buying him Indian takeaways, tidying up his caravan.

"Eventually, things went from bad to worse. The DHSS caught up with me, and I ended up in a lot of trouble. My parents were furious. It was like my worst nightmare come true. I realised then what a complete fool I'd been — I had half an education and a whole lot of hassle. Even Nathan wasn't worth this.

"Things are better now. I'm at college, and I still go through to help out at the carnival at weekends. Nathan got engaged to his steady girlfriend the other week, but I don't think it'll last. And I intend to be there to pick up the pieces. Nancy says I'll end up going the same way again, but I've learned my lesson. This time I won't get involved."

The Girl's Back In Town!

Trevor remembered Laura all too well . . .

A few days later . . .

But then . . .

YOU WHAT? LAURA HARPER? IT CAN'T BE. LAURA HARPER WAS A DOG. THIS GIRL'S BEAUTIFUL. WHAT'S SHE HAD — PLASTIC SURGERY?

SHE'S JUST GROWN UP, TREV, THAT'S ALL. IT'LL HAPPEN TO YOU ONE DAY.

TO THINK THAT A GORGEOUS GIRL LIKE LAURA HARPER USED TO BE CRAZY ABOUT ME! I REMEMBER SHE USED TO BE THE ROMANTIC TYPE. HMMM . . . NOW *THERE'S* AN IDEA . . .

And . . .

HI, LAURA! JUST A LITTLE PRESSIE TO WELCOME YOU BACK.

WELCOME ME BACK? BUT I DON'T UNDERSTAND . . .

YOU DON'T RECOGNISE ME, DO YOU? IT'S TREV! TREVOR WATSON!

TREVOR WATSON? OF COURSE! YOU'VE CHANGED A BIT SINCE I SAW YOU LAST.

AND I'M NOT THE ONLY ONE!

IT'S GREAT SEEING YOU AGAIN, LAURA. I'VE NEVER FORGOTTEN YOU — OR THE TIMES WE HAD, EH?

ER . . . YES. TALKING OF TIME, I'M LATE FOR A LECTURE SO I MUST DASH. CATCH YOU AROUND, OK?

YOU BET! SEE YOU, LAURA!

SHE'S LOVELY! AND TO THINK THAT I USED TO HIDE BEHIND THE SCHOOL SHEDS TO AVOID HER. WELL, THOSE DAYS ARE DEFINITELY OVER! FROM NOW ON, IT'S ME AND LAURA — TOGETHER, FOREVER!

A few days later . . .

SO HOW DO YOU FANCY AN AFTERNOON BROWSING AROUND THE SHOPS?

GREAT IDEA, SHIRLEY. WHO KNOWS, WE MIGHT EVEN SEE SOMETHING WE CAN AFFORD!

HI THERE, LAURA! FANCY BUMPING INTO YOU AGAIN!

YOU DON'T MIND IF I TAG ALONG, DO YOU?

WELL, ACTUALLY, WE WERE THINKING OF GOING SHOPPING THIS AFTERNOON, TREVOR. YOU'D BE BORED RIGID.

NAH! NOT ME. BESIDES, IF YOU'RE THINKING OF BUYING SOME NEW CLOTHES, I CAN GIVE YOU A MAN'S POINT OF VIEW, CAN'T I? PUT YOU ON THE RIGHT LINES . . .

And . . .

LAURA'S BEAUTIFUL. I'M A REALLY LUCKY GUY!

WHERE SHALL WE GO NEXT? HOW ABOUT THE HIGH STREET BOUTIQUES?

WHY NOT? ESPECIALLY AS TREVOR SEEMS HAPPY ENOUGH TO CARRY ALL THE BAGS . . .

That evening . . .

I'M LOOKING FORWARD TO SEEING THIS FILM. EVERYONE'S BEEN RAVING ABOUT IT.

YEAH, IT SHOULD BE GOOD.

HI, THERE, GIRLS! WE MEET AGAIN!

TREVOR! WHAT ARE YOU DOING HERE?

I'VE BEEN WANTING TO SEE THIS FILM FOR AGES. IT'S JUST LUCKY I REMEMBERED YOU WERE COMING HERE TONIGHT. WE CAN ALL SIT TOGETHER NOW. SHARE POPCORN EXPENSES, EH?

TERRIFIC . . .

continued on page 88

THE PERFECT FACE

LORI KNEW THAT GOING OUT WITH AN ARTIST WOULDN'T BE ALL MOONLIGHT AND ROSES, BUT SHE DIDN'T CARE. SHE KNEW THAT NO-ONE COULD COME BETWEEN HER AND ALAN . . .

IF Lori had worried about every girl that Alan looked at, she would have had a nervous breakdown within two months. But, fortunately, Lori was not the jealous type — and she knew instinctively that Alan wasn't interested in any of them. There were always girls around Lori and Alan — portraits leisurely sketched on scraps of paper; faint pencil roughs drawn in haste on the back of a book, or a magazine, or even, in desperation, on the inside of a chocolate wrapper. Right from the start, Alan had been searching for the perfect face.

They had met in Lori's first year at art college. Alan was in the year above her, but they still saw a lot of each other around the college. He was good-looking in a quiet sort of way; brown-haired with a soft floppy fringe, and dark grey eyes. But Lori had never noticed him until she saw the portrait he'd put in the End of Term art exhibition.

It was a strange painting. She was a green-complexioned, dark-eyed creature from outer space, obviously alien, but totally beautiful in a weird sort of way. The odd facial contours, the decidedly foreign tilt to her head — but somehow you knew that, in whatever world she came from, she was stunningly lovely. She had everyone mesmerised.

Finally Lori looked away from the portrait, and she saw a boy standing watching her. She had seen him about the college, and she knew instinctively that the painting was his. She smiled at him.

"I don't fancy bumping into her on a dark night," she said.

Alan smiled. "You won't," he assured her. "She isn't real."

"Maybe not." Lori looked at her again. "But she must be the perfect specimen, wherever she comes from."

Alan shook his head. "Oh no, not perfect. She has to be real to be perfect."

Lori looked at him with interest; he looked at her with interest; they went for a coffee and that was the start of everything.

Within a few months, Lori could hardly remember a time when Alan wasn't a part of her life. It didn't seem possible to her that it could ever end. She sometimes wondered, with a little smile, what Alan would do if he ever found his perfect face, but it didn't ever disturb her. Deep down, she didn't believe he would ever find what he was looking for. Such a thing didn't exist.

Life went on as usual — lectures, trips, holidays . . . Somehow, when Lori looked back on that time, it seemed as if the sun was always shining.

Then one day, Lori noticed that everything Alan drew these days seemed to be the same face. To begin with, she had been just one more pretty girl on another sheet of paper — suddenly she was everywhere.

"Who's this?" Lori asked one evening, deliberately trying to keep her voice casual.

"Who?" Alan asked, equally casual — but he knew who she meant. Lori picked up the sketch book and showed it to him. "Her."

He'd started a pencil sketch and tried to colour it in pastels. She had glossy, bobbed brown hair and wide brown eyes; but he'd abandoned it and gone on to another sketch. On the next page was another angle of her face — something slightly different about the tilt of her nose, the shape of her eyebrows. That too had been abandoned.

"Oh, that was just someone I saw. It won't come out right."

Lori turned over the pages of the sketchbook. It was full of

drawings of the girl. Sometimes walking, standing, laughing — sometimes he hadn't even shown her face.

"Someone you saw?" she repeated, feeling the awakening of fear inside her.

"Just a girl."

"Probably when you see her again you'll wonder what you saw in her!" Really, it was more of a question than a statement, but Alan didn't answer. His silence unnerved Lori, and she asked, "Was she pretty?"

Alan answered her without looking up. "It was the perfect face."

He didn't give up trying to recapture her. Time after time he almost got it right, but all he really had was the glossy hair and the deep bright eyes.

Lori grew to hate and fear her, that faceless girl, because she out of all the others had come between her and Alan. And she was terrified of what would happen if he found her again.

He did, of course. Too late, Lori had realised that it was something more than artistic zeal driving him on in search of her.

In the end, it was Lori who recognised her first. She had on a heavy biker's jacket and her head was bowed against the driving Autumn wind, but Lori knew her at once. She knew the shape of her eyes, screwed up against the flying leaves, the angle of her shoulders, the bounce of her hair. She'd have known her anywhere.

They were walking back from college, hurrying back to Alan's flat for rolls and hot soup. In a moment they could have passed her by and never seen her again.

Lori never knew what made her stop so suddenly and gaze at the girl. It was a conscious act, seeming almost to happen in slow motion. Perhaps it was because

SHORT STORY

she wouldn't have been able to carry on her life with Alan knowing she had prevented him finding what he wanted most.

"Alan!" Lori grabbed his sleeve. "It's her!"

It didn't register at first. But then realisation dawned in his eyes and he looked where Lori was pointing. She was walking towards him, her hair tangled by the wind. And as she lifted her eyes and found him staring, the light seemed to leap into her face. *The* eyes, the hair — he'd almost *got* it

right, in every sketch he'd *attempted*.

But she wasn't beautiful. As she stood staring, Lori felt hope coming back. She'd been right. The elusive something he'd been searching for just didn't exist. She was a pretty girl, certainly — but her chin was perhaps a little too square, her mouth was too wide. She wasn't beautiful at all. It wasn't a perfect face.

Lori turned to Alan, careful not to let her relief show in her face. But then she saw the look on

Alan's. In a split second she realised where she had been mistaken. Alan hadn't been looking for *a* prefect face — he'd been looking for *the* perfect face — *his* perfect face. Because it had to be real to be perfect.

The girl looked at Alan and smiled. He took a step towards her, and she stopped. They met like strangers, but as Lori turned to walk away, she knew that they had come together for life.

THE END

87

The following day . . .

I'D HAVE REALLY ENJOYED THAT FILM LAST NIGHT IF TREVOR HADN'T SAT THROUGH MOST OF IT UNWRAPPING TOFFEES! IT TOOK THE EDGE OFF THE REALLY ROMANTIC BITS . . .

HEY, LAURA! WAIT FOR ME!

TREVOR? WHERE DID YOU COME FROM?

OH . . . I, EM, OFTEN WALK THIS WAY TO COLLEGE. IT'S A BIT OF A SHORT CUT. I DIDN'T THINK WE'D BUMP INTO EACH OTHER, THOUGH. WHAT A COINCIDENCE.

EVEN IF I HAVE BEEN WAITING ROUND THE CORNER FOR THE LAST HALF-HOUR!

WILL YOU BE AT THE YOUTH CLUB TONIGHT?

I'M NOT SURE. I . . . EM . . . MIGHT BE STAYING IN THIS EVENING. I'VE GOT A LOT OF TECH. WORK TO CATCH UP WITH.

That evening . . .

HI, LAURA! I THOUGHT YOU MIGHT GET BORED STAYING IN ON YOUR OWN, SO I BROUGHT ROUND SOME RECORDS TO CHEER YOU UP.

OH, EM, THAT'S GREAT, TREVOR. YOU'D, ER, BETTER COME IN THEN, I SUPPOSE . . .

YOU'LL LIKE THIS ONE. IT'S MY FAVOURITE. BIG COUNTRY.

TERRIFIC . . .

I DON'T WANT TO OFFEND TREVOR. I SUPPOSE HE'S MAKING A BIG EFFORT TO BE FRIENDLY . . .

Next day . . .

LAURA'S REALLY SPECIAL, JOHN. I THINK I MUST BE IN LOVE THIS TIME . . .

SO YOU'VE ASKED HER OUT, THEN?

WELL, NO. NOT EXACTLY. NOT YET. Y'SEE, I THOUGHT SHE MIGHT BE WORRIED THAT I STILL DIDN'T FANCY HER, SO I'M EASING HER IN GENTLY, SO TO SPEAK.

LOOK, TREVOR, I DIDN'T WANT TO SAY THIS BUT, ACCORDING TO SHIRLEY, YOU'RE COMING ON A BIT STRONG. APPARENTLY, LAURA'S NOT THAT KEEN, AND . . .

WHAT ARE YOU TRYING TO SAY? THAT SHE DOESN'T FANCY ME ANY MORE?

WELL — SOMETHING LIKE THAT, YEAH.

THAT SHOWS HOW MUCH YOU KNOW, DOESN'T IT, MATE? YOU'RE JUST JEALOUS BECAUSE THE BEST-LOOKING GIRL IN COLLEGE FANCIES ME AND NOT YOU!

DON'T TALK DAFT! I'M JUST *TELLING* YOU FOR YOUR OWN *GOOD.* I DON'T WANT TO SEE YOU *MAKE* A FOOL OF YOURSELF, THAT'S ALL.

ME? MAKE A FOOL OF MYSELF? WHAT DOES JOHN KNOW ABOUT IT, ANYWAY? LAURA'S ALWAYS BEEN CRAZY ABOUT ME. I KNOW! I'LL ASK HER OUT THIS AFTERNOON. I'D LIKE TO SEE JOHN'S FACE THEN!

And . . .

HI, THERE, LAURA! GUESS WHO?

OH!

AS IF I NEED TO GUESS! TREVOR — AGAIN!

TREVOR, YOU TURN UP EVERYWHERE! DON'T YOU HAVE A HOME TO GO TO? A LIFE OF YOUR OWN TO LEAD?

SURE, BUT I'D RATHER SPEND MY TIME WITH YOU. THAT'S WHAT BEING TOGETHER'S ALL ABOUT, ISN'T IT?

TOGETHER? WHAT ARE YOU TALKING ABOUT? ARE YOU TRYING TO GET YOUR OWN BACK ON ME 'COS, IF YOU ARE, YOU'VE SUCCEEDED!

GET MY OWN BACK ON YOU? I DON'T UNDERSTAND. WHAT'RE YOU TALKING ABOUT, LAURA?

LOOK, TREVOR, I KNOW I USED TO FOLLOW YOU AROUND AT SCHOOL, BUT THAT WAS YEARS AGO. NOW YOU'RE DOING THE SAME TO ME!

LAURA — WHAT ARE YOU TRYING TO SAY?

THAT TIMES HAVE CHANGED. I DON'T FANCY YOU ANY MORE. IT WAS YEARS AGO. WE'RE DIFFERENT PEOPLE NOW.

THERE'S NOTHING BETWEEN US. THERE NEVER WAS, TREVOR. IN FACT, TO BE HONEST, THE ONLY GUY I FANCY AROUND HERE IS . . . WELL . . . JOHN!

JOHN?

YEAH. LOOK, I'M SORRY, BUT THAT'S THE WAY IT IS. AS FAR AS YOU AND I ARE CONCERNED, IT'S OVER, OK?

OVER? IT'S NOT, THOUGH, IS IT? BECAUSE IT NEVER REALLY BEGAN. I'VE BEEN A RIGHT WALLY. JOHN TRIED TO WARN ME BUT I WAS TOO FULL OF MYSELF TO LISTEN. WELL, I'VE LEARNT THE HARD WAY NOW. SOMETIMES, THERE'S JUST NO GOING BACK . . .

THE END

YOU ARE WHAT YOU EAT!

Think about what you're eating the next time you're about to tuck into french fries, hamburger and milk shake. What are you doing to your body?

If you eat too much of one thing, no matter what it is, you'll end up resembling it, whether it's a piece of lettuce; all limp and colourless, or a hamburger; a bit bumpy and full of grease!

A BALANCED DIET

There, we've said it — you'll have heard it a million times before but a balanced diet really is the best thing for you. It doesn't mean you have to eat 'rabbit food' like lettuce and carrots all the time, just have them sometimes instead of greasy things like crisps, chips and fries.

When you eat healthily, you feel healthy and you'll look great. Your complexion will improve, your hair will gleam and you'll feel more confident about yourself.

When you don't eat properly you'll tend to feel weak, tired and irritable, and your friends will love you if you're a nark all the time, won't they!?

DIETING

Dieting can be bad for you if you're not sensible about it. Don't go overboard on your first day — you can't lose three stones all at once, so take it easy!

You might think that eating very little will help you lose weight — it won't! Your body just ends up burning off fewer calories to conserve energy, then the hunger pangs begin and it's time to raid the fridge!

EATING

If you do feel the urge to eat, eat the right things and avoid the blubber.

Contrary to popular belief, healthy food can be tasty with all sorts of yummy combinations — crispbread with low fat cheese, lettuce and tomato, mmm! mmm!, followed by mixed fruit salad with apples, oranges, kiwi fruit, pineapple and cherries — scrummy!

Even snacks can be good for you — if you feel guilty at the mere sight of a Mars Bar, don't worry, there are loads of things which are relatively fat and sugar free, like unsweetened popcorn, muesli bars and oatcakes with honey.

WATER

Almost 80% of your body is water so, to feel and look healthy, this must be kept constant.

On a normal day, the body loses five or six pints of water and, if this isn't replaced, the cells will become dehydrated. Just think of a dried up potato — not a pretty sight, is it? That's what you'll end up like without replacing the fluid.

You should drink at least eight glasses of water a day to flush all of the harmful toxins and wastes from your body. You'll probably be able to tell if you're not drinking enough water because you'll feel tired and very spotty!

DRINKING

There are lots of drinks, some common, some a bit strange, so there'll be something for everyone.

On winter days, when you've been out having a snow fight, you'll murder a hot drink, but it needn't be sweetening hot chocolate or coffee with the whole of the world's sugar supply in it!

Try having flavoured and fruit teas (they can be iced in summer) that don't need sugar or milk. There are loads of flavours to choose from — Raspberry, Lemon, Camomile, Mango, Peppermint. Apart from being healthy and tasty, the teas are very calming and relaxing and are great at suppertime.

CHOCOLATE

Aargh! The dreaded stuff gets everywhere, doesn't it!?

Chocolate must be about the worst thing we could possibly eat — it also happens to be the most tasty, delicious, scrumptious and yummy thing too!

We counted up some of the yummiest chocolate bars to see just how many calories were in them and we got quite a shock!

Creme Egg	175
Crunchie	195
Dairy Milk	210
Double Decker	235
Fruit & Nut	245
Marathon	315
Mars Bar	295
Polo (each)	25
Toffee Crisp	245
Yorkie	360

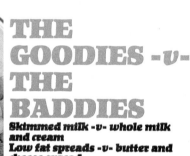

THE GOODIES -v- THE BADDIES

Skimmed milk -v- whole milk and cream
Low fat spreads -v- butter and cheese spread
Beans -v- potatoes full of starch
Bananas, apples, oranges, pears -v- Mars Bars, Marathons
Crispbread, French toast, Dutch Crispbakes -v- chocolate Hob-Nobs
Low fat cheese, cottage cheese -v- full fat French cheeses like Brie
Grilled food -v- food fried in half a ton of cooking fat
Low calorie mayonnaise -v- salad cream splurged all over a tiny piece of cucumber
Sunflower oil -v- cooking fat and dripping. Urgh!!

VEGETARIANISM

Eating healthily for some people means going without meat.

Vegetarianism is a controversial issue and it's up to you whether you want to do without meat or not. It has its advantages and disadvantages — vegetarians are at less risk from heart disease as they eat less fat, however they also lose out on a lot of vitamins and minerals which are necessary.

Vitamins aren't exactly the first thing on your mind when you're about to tuck into something tasty, but they are important.

Without these, the vegetarian can suffer from anaemia, weak bones, lank hair and dull skin.

You might also find that you'll suffer from severe period pains and pre-menstrual tension.

EAT WELL, FEEL WELL

After your Christmas dinner (and 392 selection boxes) you'll probably feel sick at the mere sight of food. However, once you get back into the munching mode try to control what you eat — that means no strict (bordering on starvation) diets and no bingeing on chocolate for you, matey!

OH NO, NOT ANOTHER MATHS TEST!

NUMEROLOGY dates back as far as numbers themselves and has quite an interesting history. In ancient Greece, the alphabet was used to denote numbers — alpha, 1; beta, 2; gamma, 3; etc — as it also was in Judea — aleph, 1; beth, 2; gimel, 3; etc. During the middle ages, scholars tried to use a system called *Gematria* to replace words in cryptic passages of the Bible with others of the same numeric value. This didn't lead to any spectacular revelations but kept them busy during the long winter nights.

Modern numerology has little in common with *Gematria*, although many books use what they call the "Hebrew system". This is a bit of a misnomer as they use the English alphabet and Arabic numerals . . . so there's not really anything Hebron about it!

In some people's eyes, numerology is a science and is as reliable as, say, quantum physics. But there again, most of quantum physics is theoretical and theories are nothing more than educated guesses. It stands to reason, then, that they can often be astoundingly wrong! The numbers in your name and date of birth aren't going to tell us much about the future, but perhaps they can hint at your personality and your weak points. From there, it's up to you to make the most of what you've got. . .

THE LETTERS . . . AND NUMBERS

1	2	3	4	5	6	7	8	9
A	B	C	D	E	F	G	H	I
J	K	L	M	N	O	P	Q	R
S	T	U	V	W	X	Y	Z	

The block of numbers and letters should be self-explanatory. If it isn't, all that needs to be said in the way of explanation is that the numbers at the top of each column are to be taken as the numerical value of the letters in that column. Therefore, A=1, M=4, J=1, R=9, and so on. Got that? Good!

Now, let's take the name TRACEY SMITH as an example here. To find the numerical value of this name, all we have to do is add up the letters so we're left with a single figure.

e.g.

$$T R A C E Y \qquad S M I T H$$
$$2+9+1+3+5+7 \qquad 1+4+9+2+8$$
$$=27 \qquad\qquad =24$$
$$2+7 \qquad\qquad 2+4$$
$$=9 \qquad\qquad =6$$
$$9+6$$
$$=15$$
$$1+5$$
$$=6$$

What we now know is that the number which equals the name TRACEY SMITH is 6.

Now, let's say that TRACEY SMITH was born on March 26 1976. By adding up all the numbers in her date of birth, we can find another number.

e.g.

$$3+(2+6)+(1+9+7+6)$$
$$3+8+5$$
$$=16=(1+6)=7$$

We now have two numbers for our imaginary friend, *6* and *7*. If we wanted, we could add them together and come up with another number (4), but we already have enough to work with for the moment.

By this time, you're probably wondering what these numbers tell us about TRACEY SMITH. It's all very well knowing that someone is *sixy* or *sevenish*, but it would be far more useful knowing what these qualities are. First of all, let's look at the positive aspects . . .

+POINTS

1. This is a particulary masculine *number in as much as it stands for qualities like courage, leadership and* independence. The ONE person is very much a doer and can be relied upon to see things through to the finish and to encourage others.

2. TWO is, traditionally, the opposite of ONE, i.e. it expresses the feminine qualities of tact, wisdom and gentleness. The TWO person is a perfect home-maker and can use their natural wiles to create ease and harmony in any environment.

3. The THREE person is a natural-born entertainer, whether it be through performing, writing or speaking, and will not be happy unless they're bringing joy to others.

4. FOUR people are very determined, strong-willed and reliable. They're prepared to work hard, notice every detail and make good friends.

5. FIVE is the number of the free spirit. The FIVE person excels in communication and loves to drift from place to place, idea to idea.

6. SIX denotes romance. The SIX person sees beauty everywhere and is caring, responsible and artistic. Their ideal is to settle down in their own little nest and be content.

7. SEVEN is a spook number. The SEVEN person is solitary, secretive and a bit of a philosopher. Creatively, the SEVENS are in a league of their own and can be seen as 'weird' by others. They are often a source of inspiration to others, but tend to keep their 'secrets' to themselves.

8. EIGHT is usually a good sign of business-sense. EIGHT people are ambitious but usually have the ability to match. They are suited to decisive business matters and are very practically-minded. It is also a number associated with marriage.

9. NINE is the sign of a great deal of energy. People with this number are capable of putting their natural drive and intuition to good use. They have a lot of tolerance and can show their judgment and compassion, even under pressure. They make good leaders.

11. ELEVEN is a special number and is thought of as being the sign that someone has discovered the truth about themselves and are at ease with their individuality. They are normally loners and inspire awe in others.

What we can deduce from this is that our subject, TRACEY SMITH, is romantic, artistic, a bit of a dreamer, and rather secretive about herself, but can be jealous, narrow-minded, and is not too emotionally secure. This is all fine and well, but, since she's only an imaginary person, we can't tell whether she is like that or not, can we? Well, what about these people here? They're all pretty well known, but do they fit in with what their names say about them?

NAME: Prince — 11 or 12
REAL NAME: Nelson Rogers —8
DATE OF BIRTH: 7/6/1960 — 11 or 2
Shrewd businessman with a great deal of insight. He's definitely in a league of his own and leaves his competitors in the shade. His entourage of beautiful women is proof of his gentleness and understanding. Consider his negative aspects for yourself . . .

NAME: Marilyn Monroe — 1
REAL NAME: Norma Jean Baker — 11 or 2
Date of Birth: 1/6/1926 — 7
Courageous and independent, with all the natural feminine wiles. A great inspiration for both men and women. In real life she lacked confidence and had a drink problem, and her submissiveness led to her untimely death.

NAME: Madonna — 4
REAL NAME: Madonna Ciccone — 11 or 2
DATE OF BIRTH: 16/8/1958 — 11 or 2
She's in her own little world and makes everyone want to join her in it. She's also worked very hard for what she's got and is respected throughout her profession. On the other hand, she's a bit of a rebel and flits from one 'job' to another without considering the effects on her career.

NAME: Bono — 1
REAL NAME: Paul Hewson — 8
DATE OF BIRTH: 27/5/1957 — 4
Another businessman with great leadership qualities. His determination has made him one of the world's biggest stars. His egotism could cause him problems, though.

NAME: Johnny Rotten — 7
REAL NAME: John Lydon — 9
DATE OF BIRTH: 31/1/1956
He's still regarded as the leader of the punk generation and his energy is not in question. His business acumen brought off "The Great Rock 'n' Roll Swindle" but the self-indulgence, which claimed some of his contemporaries, almost claimed him.

What do you think, then? Try the system out on yourself and your friends . . . even if it doesn't reveal any secrets, it could be fun! It's far better than maths, anyway!

—ASPECTS

1. ONES can be lazy, lack confidence in themselves, be indecisive or, at the other extreme, over-confident, egotistical and quick-tempered . . . or any other major failing that men usually display!

2. TWOS can be submissive, fussy, over-emotional, moody and 'conservative' . . . some of the worst traits of women!

3. THREES can sometimes be pessimists and cynics and are often unprepared to see anything through to its completion.

4. FOURS can be rebellious and destructive. They can also be stubborn, unreliable, careless and prone to let their minds wander.

5. FIVES can be destructive, deceitful and irresponsible. They are fraudulent and are good liars.

6. SIXES can be narrow-minded, jealous and quarrelsome. They can be over-possessive about their loved ones.

7. SEVENS can often become disillusioned with their beliefs and may fall into problems with drink, drugs or illness, due to their inability to cope with reality.

8. EIGHTS can be over-dependent on others and can suffer if they drive themselves too hard or neglect their own interests for the sake of their goal.

9. NINES can be narrow-minded and selfish and allow this to influence their dealings with others.

11. ELEVENS can be slightly strange due to their "unearthly" qualities and are vulnerable to con-men.

94